THE COAL RIVER VALLEY
IN THE
CIVIL WAR

MICHAEL B. GRAHAM

THE COAL RIVER VALLEY
IN THE
CIVIL WAR

West Virginia Mountains, 1861

THE
History
PRESS

Published by The History Press
Charleston, SC 29403
www.historypress.net

Front cover, top right: Union colonel Abraham (Abram) S. Piatt, commander, Thirty-Fourth Ohio Infantry Regiment, led the Federal force that was victorious in the Battle of Kanawha Gap on September 25, 1861. *Taken from* Ohio in the War *(1868)*.

First published 2014

Manufactured in the United States

ISBN 978.1.62619.660.5

Library of Congress CIP data applied for.

Private Philip Roush, Company D, 141st Ohio Infantry
Private Andrew Sayre, Company H, 3rd West Virginia Cavalry
Private Thomas W. Steele, Company G, 3rd West Virginia Cavalry
Dr. George A. Vandelinde, Surgeon, 187th Regiment (Boone), Virginia State Militia

Lest we forget

Contents

FOREWORD

I've known Mike Graham since we both worked for the old U.S. Information Agency (now part of the Department of State) during the 1980s, so I was delighted when he asked me to write an introduction to his book. We both were active in an informal military history discussion group, made up of USIA employees, that met for lunch on occasion to talk about our own historical research or some pre-selected military history topic. Later, I invited Mike to speak to the Loudoun County (Virginia) Civil War Roundtable, of which I was then president, about the river campaigns early in the war in western Virginia. I know of no one who is better equipped than he to tackle the topic of this current book.

One of the joys of doing Civil War research is that, despite there being over sixty thousand books and innumerable articles already written on the subject, it is always possible to find some small niche that has yet to be explored. That is one of the values of delving into local history as well. Combine the two, and we have a perfect example of why a book like *The Coal River Valley in the Civil War: West Virginia Mountains, 1861* is so useful and will always be so welcome an addition to the literature of the Civil War.

The western portion of Virginia, and the fighting that occurred therein, is one such niche study. Isolated by mountains and distant from the center of political, economic and social activity in Virginia, the region never quite seemed to fit, and movements to split it off into a separate state long predated the Civil War. It certainly is understandable that the people of Wheeling, Virginia, would have felt a much greater identification, and even kinship, with the people of Pittsburgh, only sixty miles away, than they would have felt with the people of Richmond, which was four hundred miles and several mountain ranges away. It was this isolated position and the fact that the actions occurred so early in the war that make the story of what happened in the area still fairly unknown, obscure and underappreciated.

It does not help that there were no epic battles to focus the attention of the press. Indeed, such battles as there were would more appropriately be called skirmishes, especially by later war standards. As the author points out, the total casualties over the period covered in the book—not much more than a month—barely reaches three hundred. Nevertheless, this series of fights and troop movements contributed in a big way toward establishing Federal control over the region. That, in turn, allowed for the development of the generally unmolested political movement that eventually resulted in the creation of the state of West Virginia. A similar movement for separate statehood in eastern Tennessee failed precisely because Federal forces were unable to establish that kind of military control. Thus, today, there is a state of West Virginia but no state of East Tennessee. That demonstrates the importance of this series of small, local fights.

The Coal River Valley, and Boone County in particular, was a microcosm of Virginia and of the country as a whole. Mike effectively describes the divisions between political factions and between families, divisions that so often overlapped, thereby setting the scene for the often vicious behaviors shown by each side toward the other over and above the actual military encounters. It was often literally brother against brother, not unusual during the Civil War, but particularly noticeable on the small scale and in the local settings discussed in this book. "Bloody Kansas" has nothing on the western portion of Virginia in that regard.

Mike goes on to discuss, in clarifying detail, the troop movements and battles that occurred, giving them the chronological coherence that is so important, especially with actions that will not likely be well known to readers, even to most Civil War enthusiasts. The same is true of the main characters in the story, men who are important in this context but whose names generally do not appear in the larger story of the war. As someone who has himself written on a small, obscure, early war fight, I particularly appreciate Mike's ability to bring these men to life.

The Coal River Valley in the Civil War: West Virginia Mountains, 1861 is a book that needed to be written. For those with a focused interest on early war activities, it will be especially useful. For the general reader, it will provide good historical background and an increased understanding of the greater difficulties to be found in the border warfare of the period.

I am pleased to highly recommend this book to anyone with an interest in America's defining moment.

JAMES A. MORGAN III
author of *A Little Short of Boats: The Civil War Battles of Ball's Bluff and Edwards Ferry, October 21–22, 1861*

Acknowledgements

The list of people who helped with this work is a lengthy one. Certainly, the late geologist and founder of the Boone County (West Virginia) Genealogical Society, Sigfus "Sig" Olafson (1897–1987), was an inspiration for this book. Sig Olafson, with whom I became associated as a newspaperman for the region's principal local newspaper, the *Coal Valley News*, was a coal and gas surveyor and friend of my grandfather Denver D. Roush, longtime town manager and the fire and police chief of Madison, West Virginia. As a surveyor, Sig came in frequent contact with the people of Boone County. He became interested in genealogy after reading the many deeds and wills that he was required to research for his surveying work. As a result, through his careful research and writings, he established himself as "the expert" on Boone County history and genealogy, writing many articles that appeared in the *Coal Valley News*, publications of the Boone County Genealogical Society and numerous national historical, geological, archaeological and genealogical works.

Another inspiration for this book was the great Civil War historian Dr. Bell Irvin Wiley (1906–1980), the first to examine the war from the common soldier's perspective. He found that Confederate and Federal soldiers alike relied on courage to overcome fear and "felt that it was better to die facing the enemy in battle than to flee and face the humiliation and shame of their cowardly acts." In addition to providing a young undergraduate history student patient counsel and encouragement, the famous author of classic Civil War books such as *Johnny Reb* (1943) and *Billy Yank* (1952) drew my attention to the special Civil War historical collection of Marshall University's John W. Morrow Library. This led me to Boyd B. Stutler's authoritative book *West Virginia in the Civil War* (1963), which contained then the most (in fact, only) published historical account of the burning of Boone Court House, an event that is central to understanding how the Civil War unfolded in southern West Virginia and that also says much about aspects of human nature.

Fellow Civil War historian James A. Morgan III, past president of the Loudoun County (Virginia) Civil War Roundtable, generously agreed to write the foreword to this work. Jim's tactical study, *A Little Short of Boats: The Civil War Battles of Ball's Bluff and Edwards Ferry, October 21–22, 1861* (2011), is widely acclaimed as the definitive work on Ball's Bluff. Jim also penned a splendid artillery unit history titled *Always Ready, Always Willing: A History of Battery M, Second United States Artillery from Its Organization through the Civil War* (1989). I also want to thank fellow Civil War researcher and history enthusiast Alex Snow for lending his expertise. A personal friend, conversationalist and expert authority on the war in his own right (especially the Battle of Gettysburg and the Eighth Virginia Cavalry Regiment), Alex's depth of Civil War historical knowledge, his suggestions for developing the material and his assistance in securing some of the needed research documentation in order to tell the story as completely as possible were indispensable to the success of this project.

Special acknowledgement must be made for the help of Hal Jespersen, who undertook the professional development of the cartography of the events described in this work. This is the first time these battles have ever been mapped, and Hal's impressive skills were instrumental in preparing publishable quality maps from my crude sketches. In short, to all of these colleagues, my heartfelt thanks to all in the hope that this book will stimulate greater interest in and appreciation and use of their works. Thanks also to Lawrence D. Roush, National Park Service (ret.), and my uncle, for his assistance with some of the genealogical research. And to Banks Smither, my commissioning editor, and project editor Will Collicott, both professionals at The History Press, for their tenacity, ingenuity and good humor displayed throughout the process. Many others, too numerous to cite, contributed in abundant ways both large and small throughout the decades.

Throughout this work, primary and secondary published and manuscript material from government, military and individual service records; newspapers; the research of local historians and genealogical researchers; biographies; battles and campaigns studies; regimental histories; personal accounts and memoirs; general and county histories; and reunions and veterans organizations, as well as anecdotes, family recollections and oral tradition (abbreviated OT), are cited in the notes. These sources appear in full in the bibliography. Reference to material in *The War of the Rebellion: A Compilation of the Official Records of the Union and Confederate Armies* is abbreviated as *OR*; unless otherwise noted, all references are to Series 1.

References to Union army units attributable to the region now known as the state of West Virginia are indicated as "(West) Virginia" before June 20, 1863, the date of West Virginia's statehood. Prior to that date, the region was still officially part of Virginia. After statehood, such units are indicated as "West Virginia."

Introduction

I find it extremely interesting that the passage of more than 150 years has increased curiosity about the historical events and personalities that this book describes. No wonder—the story has never been told. There is not another single volume of American Civil War history focused on the events that occurred in the Coal River Valley, the second-largest river system in the state of West Virginia. It has been mentioned in passing by a few historians but has never been seriously, or even very carefully, examined. At best, it was vaguely preserved through oral traditions not fully filled in because today we know so much more about the Civil War.

In fact, I had the good fortune to grow up, for the most part, in Boone County, West Virginia, the epicenter of most of the events described in this book. My family's roots there are deep, going back to the earliest settlers in the valley in the late 1700s. A fourth great-grandfather figured prominently in the events this book describes. Dying of tuberculosis shortly after the war, he and tens of thousands like him who died after the war from causes connected to their military service might have lived long and abundant lives if not for their service. They were as much casualties as those who fell on the battlefields. His wife and his young sons, though, witnessed the comings and goings of the Union and Confederate armies through the valley, and snippets of their harrowing reminiscences filtered down through the generations that followed. And yet even much later, in my time, the war in the Coal River Valley was not much talked about openly. The schools did not teach it. Certainly, little was written about it. The subject was taboo; therefore, it was unusual to hear much about it. It was still too sensitive to discuss—over one hundred years later.

Of course, it was commonly known that the Union army burned Boone Court House during the war, although the reason why and the circumstances surrounding the memorable event were fuzzy or had been forgotten. In addition, there was an intriguing folktale about the wandering ghost of a headless Civil War soldier. It concerns a fierce battle that occurred in the Big Coal River country near present-day Bloomingrose. "Some say," as the story goes, the ghost of a headless Union soldier who was killed there haunts the riverbanks in search of his head.[1] But how or why the soldier lost his head was not explained in the storytelling. Or why this family or that family, even whole communities, over one hundred years after the war were characterized as "Yankees" or "Johnnies." Or why the rivalries of clans, towns and school sports teams in the region remain so intense. And so on.

The fact is that West Virginia had mixed loyalties. As many of its men served the South as they did the North, probably more. Although not a major battleground during the war, brutal guerrilla activity and continuous raiding by both sides kept the region constantly in violent turmoil. The period in the Mountain State from 1861 through 1865 was fraught with confusion, upheaval and uncertainty for the citizens of both warring sides.

Foremost, the complicated nature of the war itself in the mountains has been a notable deterrent even to understanding it. Over twenty-four thousand square miles in size, twice the size of Maryland and equal to New Hampshire, New Jersey and Connecticut combined, this wilderness area of operations betwixt the eastern and western theaters of the war makes it difficult to comprehend the course of the war there. A study of the war there involves many hundreds of events, mostly small, unconnected affairs fought at far distances from one another seemingly without much relation. As Mark Twain's Connecticut Yankee observed, "When you come to figure up results, you can't tell one fight from another, nor who whipped; and as a picture, of living, raging, roaring battle, sho! why, it's pale and noiseless—just ghosts scuffling in a fog."[2]

However, for a brief time in August–September 1861—for a period of less than thirty days—the armies of North and South in the struggle for what was then western Virginia were vitally concerned with this watershed region of 890 square miles of backwoods mountain wilderness etched with hundreds of miles of rivers and creeks. The struggle, especially along the Big and Little Forks of the Coal River and their main tributaries, was bitter and savage. With the revived interest in Civil War history today, I expect that this work will appeal to every kind of reader, young and old—those interested in not only the special role and place of the great state of West Virginia in the Civil War but also the strategy, raiding, guerrilla warfare and terrorism that occurred in the mountains.

I will be especially pleased if this book is the last clever item that is stuffed into the backpacks of tourists and wilderness enthusiasts before they embark on adventure outings along the entire eighty-eight miles of the Big Coal, Little Coal and Coal Rivers to explore the beautiful mountains and waterways while hiking, hunting, fishing, four-wheeling and boating or canoeing. Genealogists will be drawn to the book's material because of what it tells them about ancestry. It is a tribute to those insufficiently appreciated souls whose vast contributions to Civil War history have made it worthwhile to issue this work.

Because of my lifelong interest in and research of West Virginia's Civil War history, I occasionally have been asked to lecture. Some of the material herein supported a guest lecture delivered before the Loudoun County (Virginia) Civil War Roundtable some years past. Today, with the upsurge of interest in the Civil War surrounding the sesquicentennial commemoration, new generations of Americans are discovering the war and this dimension of the nation's heritage. In addition, fresh looks are being taken at old historical assumptions as new information becomes increasingly available.

This is so today of West Virginia, too long overlooked as a forgotten part of the war, as its history during the postwar Reconstruction period and since then has managed to serve the purposes of statehood and to burnish the image of West Virginia's "secession from Secession." This is especially true of the Coal River Valley, the scene of some of the most violent internecine fighting anywhere in all the war, manifestly ignored by Civil War historians—again, except that the Boone County Courthouse was burned by Federal soldiers. The reason for this, I tend to think, is primarily because prior to the rise of the Internet and the powerful archival research tools of the Digital Age, the threadwork of the story was simply lost. The dark veil of time, however, is now slowly lifting to reveal to us new dimensions of the Civil War, preserved for over a century and half.

Foremost, while the total number of soldiers who died during the Civil War is difficult to state with precision, modern research enabled by powerful computer modeling has disclosed that the death toll from the Civil War was much higher than we thought—not 620,000 dead, as assumed since 1900, but as many as 850,000.[3] The Battle of Boone Court House in September 1861, one of the more grim and iconic events of the war in West Virginia and around which this particular book revolves, is a case in point. For over one hundred years, historians have assumed that there were about fourteen total casualties altogether on both sides. That number is proved herein to be significantly low, however. Why would that be so? The battle, after all, was a "significant engagement," as defined in Phisterer's authoritative *Chronological Record of Engagements, Battles, Etc., in the United States, 1861 to 1865.*[1]

Briefly, Boone Court House was a small affair far from the major fields of the war. The expedition was conducted by a mixture of Union troops in company formations from five separate regiments, including loosely organized militia auxiliaries and an independent artillery battery. On the Confederate side, the troops represented companies of militia from two different regiments and members of the general citizenry who were not formally enrolled in the militias. Efforts to count the casualties were impossible, as immediately after the battle, the combatant elements all went their separate ways, and their scarce reports were incomplete and inaccurate. And what of those who died after the battle from wounds that proved mortal or from disease as prisoners of war? The new estimate suggests that there likely were at least sixty-eight total casualties associated with Boone Court House, which is almost five times the traditional estimate. There were probably more than that. In other words, the battle was more costly to many more families and communities than historically assumed. This realization today helps explain why the event became such a searing and terrible moment in the region's collective memory.

Called *Walhondecepe* (pronounced Wall-hond-eh-see-pee, or "ditch place") by the Delaware Indians, the three rivers that make up the Coal River Valley—the Big, Little and Coal Rivers—were called the Louisa River by the early French trappers and later renamed the Coal by eighteenth-century explorer John Peter Salling (or Salley) for the coal deposits he observed along the banks.[5] Since humans first arrived in the region many thousands of years ago, the three rivers that make up the Coal River Valley—meandering through present-day Raleigh, Boone, Lincoln and Kanawha Counties "like a snake with two heads"—have served as a vital transportation link to the Kanawha, New and Ohio Rivers. The Indians used the valley and rivers as hunting and fishing lands.[6]

Early European settlers in the region—who came mostly from Virginia and North Carolina—discovered outcrops of cannel coal (known as candle coal) along the Big Coal River. The oil manufactured from the coal burned brightly and produced very little smoke and was used to replace whale oil for lighting. Very desirable as a source of heat and light, the cannel coal was

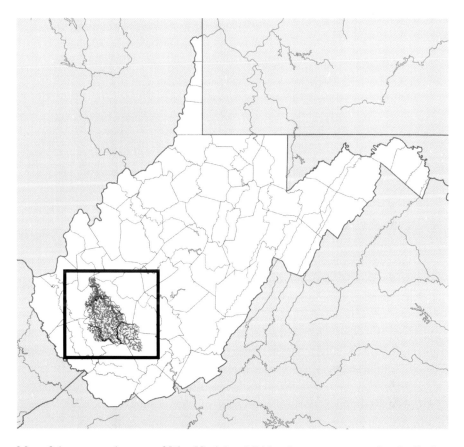

Map of the present-day state of West Virginia exhibiting the area encompassing the Coal River Valley. *Wikimedia Commons.*

shipped for sale to the growing antebellum industrial cities of Louisville, Kentucky; Cincinnati, Ohio; Wheeling, Virginia; New Orleans; New York; and Boston. The large seams of coal attracted investors to the region in the mid-1800s. The utilization of the rivers for navigation was enhanced by the construction of a public road connecting the county seats of Boone and Logan Counties to the Kanawha Valley and by the construction of a large-scale lock and dam system on the rivers.

> *In the early history of Boone, Logan and Mingo Counties nearly all the freight imported into these counties was hauled in wagons from the Kanawha River at Marmet (formerly Brownstown). This route extended from the Kanawha to the Guyandot [sic] River, near Chapmanville, along*

the creeks and across the low divides, starting at Marmet, thence going up Lens Creek and crossing the dividing ridge and down Short Creek to Racine, on Coal River; thence, down the north side of said river to the mouth of Drawdy Creek; thence, crossing the river and up Drawdy Creek and across the divide and down Rock Creek for about four miles; thence, crossing the divide to the south, to Trice Branch, and down same to Little Coal River at Danville; thence by two courses, one by way of Turtle Creek to Big Creek of Guyandot [sic] River, and the other by way of Little Coal River and Spruce Fork to mouth of Low Gap Creek, and up same to Big Creek, and thence down Big Creek for about six miles, and thence crossing the divide to Chapmanville.

Another route for southern Boone and the northern part of Wyoming Counties extends from Racine up Coal River to mouth of Laurel Creek at Seth, and up Seth Creek to mouth of Coal Fork, and up that branch to cross the divide to Whites Branch of West Fork of Coal River, and down same to Pond Fork and thence up Pond Fork.[7]

In 1851, the Coal River Navigation Company was formed to complete the construction of the lock and dam system, mostly along the Coal and Big Coal Rivers. The thirty-four-mile system contained the first working locks and dams on an inland waterway in America.[8] The system included one lock on the Little Coal River that opened five miles of that stream to steamboats and barges. Floods repeatedly washed out the lock and dam system, but investors continued to rebuild, and the system operated successfully from 1855 to 1861. One-hundred-foot-long paddlewheel steamboats navigated the rivers via the locks and dams, transporting coal barges day and night. In 1860 alone, nearly 1 million bushels of the valuable cannel coal were shipped in this manner. The abundant timber in the region was worked for building river steamboats and barges or floated to the Kanawha Valley for sale.

A report prepared for the 1893 World's Fair noted:

Before the war, that bloody period from which so many events in the South are dated, Boone county was undergoing a rapid development which has never been equaled since. Big Coal river from its mouth to Peytona, some 30 miles, was locked and dammed, making it navigable for boats and barges. A railroad several miles in length connected rich cannel coalmines with Peytona and the river and great quantities of coal were mined and shipped. Then came the war, property was destroyed, the dams were broken [and] the railroad went to decay.[9]

The Civil War indeed stopped operations of the system, but in 1867, a new company was formed, and the locks and dams returned to service. The system operated anew for sixteen years until the mid-1880s. The prewar-built system is now listed on the National Register of Historic Places. Interestingly, today the Coal River from St. Albans to Tornado remains a designated U.S. navigable waterway. It is a major kayaking and canoeing waterway.

The legacy of the Civil War is still with us, in our national consciousness, as even today the abysmal horrors unleashed in that time still resonate somewhere on a daily basis—in the vestige forms of radicalism, sectionalism, militarism of policy, racism and myriad other "isms" that so afflict the human condition. When it was decided to bring out this work, I debated whether to include the research as part of an entire book on the history of the Civil War in West Virginia or publish the material on its own. I ultimately chose the latter because I simply felt that this was a history whose time had come and that should endure on its own.

This book is essentially written as a piece of reporting capturing a historical moment. It encapsulates aspects of my decades of special interest in learning about and researching the Civil War in West Virginia. Much of it was written over the course of my life so far—a piece of information collected here, a piece gathered there, a diary or manuscript discovered, people I met with family narratives to share and the background knowledge of history absorbed and whatever experience I acquired traipsing throughout the full range of the Coal River Valley region as a youth and, later, as a newspaperman.

In addition, the war offers something about the sources of some of the historical rivalries of clans and communities in the Coal River Valley. In the period from 1861 to 1865, the region itself dissolved into chaos as state and local government and the rule of law altogether broke down, plunging the people into the descent of terror and leaving the population to fend for itself. The burning of Boone Court House (present-day Madison), an act that seemed to serve no purpose other than to inflict humiliation and terror in order to subdue the general population, is well known. However, few know that other communities in the valley were also torched and reduced to smoldering ruins by one side or the other during the campaign (present-day Bloomingrose, by the Union army, and Bald Knob, by Confederate raiders) or that a Union fort built and manned by Pond Fork militia was overrun and burned.

How the Union army, as part of its larger pursuits in the Kanawha Valley, set on securing the Coal River Valley is a historically overlooked but important part of the overall story of events with which this work is concerned. Chapter 1 provides the background of the war in West Virginia, only against which can the Coal River Valley campaign of 1861 be understood and appreciated. Here the story of action leading up to the conduct of the events is covered. The leading personalities are framed (Union general Jacob D. Cox, colonels James V. Guthrie and David A. Enyart, captain William Walker Jr., militia leader Floyd Cooke and scout William Workman; Confederate generals Henry A. Wise and John B. Floyd, colonel Ezekiel S. Miller, captain Henry Clay Pate), along with many others who were living and fighting in this nearly no-man's borderland.[10]

As the historian Creasey observed, "It is not the number of killed and wounded in a battle that determines its general historical importance."[11] The Battle of Boone Court House was the pivotal and defining event of this part of the Civil War in western Virginia in 1861. Drawing on official and historical material never used before, Chapter 2 for the first time illuminates the fateful encounter between the armies of the North and South at this Little Coal River crossroads town from August 31 to September 1. A Federal force of infantry and artillery, joined by local Union militia allies, clashed with Rebel militia. The in-depth account foreshadows the sobering consequences of the battle and its disastrous effects on the region that lasted long after the war.

Based on the *Official Records* and firsthand accounts, Chapter 3 tells the story of the Battle of Coal River, fought on September 12, 1861. Marked by brilliant strategic maneuvering, the thundering of hooves and exploits of gallantry under fire, the account of the battle illustrates the role of the Confederate cavalry arm and its flexible leadership and tactics in the mountains. A saber-swinging Confederate cavalry battalion chased down, charged and shattered a larger Federal raiding force of infantry and artillery in a running, three-mile affair along the northern shore of the Big Coal River from the mouth of Joes Creek (now called Comfort) to Toney's Branch near present-day Bloomingrose, all communities that are situated today along the current West Virginia State Route 3 highway.

From the construction of a Union fort at Walnut Gap/Skin Creek to the burning of the homes of Union militia and sympathizers in the Bald Knob area, Chapter 4 conveys the Battle of Pond Fork, September 17–18, 1861, and the boldness of colorful Federal and Confederate leaders. A Union militia company of Home Guards was surprised in its breastworks by a Confederate raiding force of cavalry, dispersed and a large number of the Federals captured. Based on the *Official Records* and applying recently available sources never before used in Civil War histories, the account relates

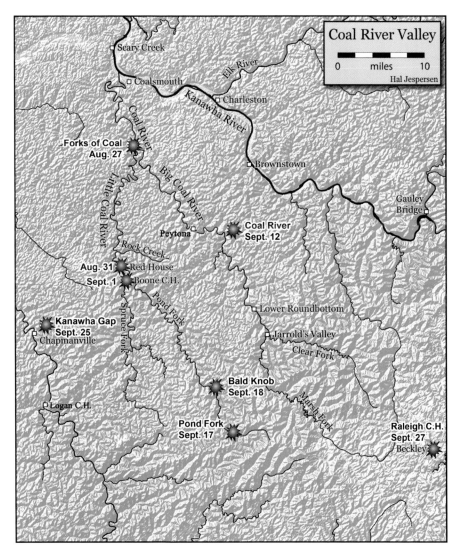

Area of significant August–September 1861 actions encompassing present-day Coal River Valley. *Author's collection.*

the stark tragedy of the captured men's pitiable saga as prisoners of war at Libby Prison in Richmond.

The Battle of Kanawha Gap, on September 25, 1861, was the culminating event. Using newly discovered eyewitness accounts and soldiers' memoirs, Chapter 5 provides the definitive fact-packed story of that day—with the possible exception of Boone Court House, the most important battle of the campaign. A Federal force of infantry and artillery came up against a Confederate cavalry company at Washington Township/Trace Fork, near present-day Manila. The resulting outcome against a Rebel militia force in mountainside entrenchments near Chapmanville crushed organized Confederate resistance in the Coal River Valley region for the balance of the war thereafter.

The remainder of the book provides commentary on generals, officers, common soldiers and ordinary citizens from both sides of the conflict caught up in the dramatic sweep and valor of this area of the war's operations that shaped southern West Virginia's history and consciousness. Finally, in the practice of history, we seek to understand the past not only to fathom the human condition but also to honor the dead—so that their lives had meaning. Although the events herein took place many years ago, through reconstructed knowledge of the past, each of us remains as a living part of the whole of time.

Any additional information about these historical events can be sent to the author in order to help in updating this history. You can contact him at tcwintcrv@gmail.com.

—Michael B. Graham

Chapter 1

PRELUDE

In the first few months of the Civil War, the South faced its first serious challenge in the mountains of western Virginia. In Washington, politicians, railroad and business interests and civilian groups urged President Abraham Lincoln and the general in chief of the U.S. Army, General Winfield Scott, to occupy western Virginia with Federal forces. Foremost, the Baltimore & Ohio (B&O) Railroad crossed the northwestern part of the region. Enormous financial investments had been made in the railroad that would be critical to moving troops and supplies in the war. Both sides foresaw the significant strategic benefits. Therefore, the North and South each coveted the B&O Railroad, and it became a guiding strategic concern of both the Union and Confederate forces.

There were other important reasons, as well, to control western Virginia. Second, occupying western Virginia would also disrupt Confederate recruiting in the region, depriving the South of a significant source of manpower for its armies. Third, occupying the region would deny the Confederacy access to the mountains' abundant strategic natural resources of coal, oil, saltpeter, wool and, especially in the Kanawha Valley, salt. Finally, for political reasons, it seemed important for the North to support the pro-Union elements among the western Virginia population disaffected with the Old Dominion.[12]

The Confederacy was similarly motivated to hold western Virginia. If the mountains could be retained, the North would be squeezed to a narrow corridor of only about one hundred miles between the Great Lakes and

West Virginia. A primary focal point early in the Civil War, both sides were anxious to control the Old Dominion's vast western mountain wilderness region. *West Virginia Department of Natural Resources.*

Virginia through which to transport western troops and supplies overland to the East. The Confederates hoped to move north and westward to take over, or at least break, the B&O Railroad that brought men and supplies eastward from Ohio, Indiana, Illinois, Michigan and Wisconsin. Finally, the South wanted to control the northwestern part of Virginia to stop the newly formed pro-Union Restored Government of Virginia at Wheeling from progressing. Throughout the region, the Confederacy initially was able to gather only a scattered token force of fewer than one thousand troops to repel invasion from Ohio and Pennsylvania and hold on to western Virginia.

In response, a general counterplan was conceived in the North. Major General George B. McClellan, in overall command of the Army of Western Virginia, would cross the Ohio River and drive out the westward-facing Confederate forces organizing to defend the region. McClellan's invasion had two wings. He directed the northern wing, while Brigadier General Jacob D. Cox directed the southern. Together, the two wings would invade and secure the region for the North. In May 1861, General McClellan, with twenty thousand men under his control, advanced from Ohio.[13]

Union major general George B. McClellan commanded the Federal army that invaded western Virginia in the summer of 1861. *Library of Congress*.

McClellan's campaign opened with startling success as the Confederates were routed in a series of brisk battles, and within six weeks, the North's conquest of northwestern Virginia was completed. For the South, the defeat of the Confederate forces was ruinous and viewed as a tremendous blow. The Union had control of both the Ohio River and the B&O Railroad.[14] The successes made McClellan a national hero and launched him to command of all the Federal armies. More importantly, the catastrophic flight of the Confederate forces enabled the work of the Union political elements in the region to continue their advancement of a new state, West Virginia, without interruption.[15]

Southward, General Cox carried out his part of the invasion of western Virginia. He crossed the Ohio River in July, landed with a brigade at

Union brigadier general Jacob D. Cox commanded the Federal forces under McClellan that invaded the Great Kanawha Valley in the summer of 1861. *Library of Congress.*

Guyandotte and continued east toward the Kanawha Valley city of Charleston.[16] Cox's force first encountered resistance at Barboursville (July 14). The Federals met six hundred Rebel militia dug in atop a ridge paralleling the Mud River and dominating the covered Mud River Bridge. The action was as sharp as it was brief. The Southern troops waited for the Federals to cross the bridge before firing, inflicting serious casualties. After an exchange of fire, the Federals conducted an uphill bayonet charge, driving the Rebels from the ridge, and took the town. Confederate losses were one mortally wounded and three to five injured, while five Federals were killed and eighteen wounded.

As Cox pressed eastward, Confederate resistance strengthened around Charleston, the center of Rebel control in the Kanawha Valley. At the crossing of Scary Creek, a tributary of the Kanawha River, Cox's leading regiments and six hundred Confederate infantry, cavalry and artillery clashed on July 17. Four hours of hard fighting were needed to drive back the Federals. Considering the number of troops engaged, Federal losses were heavy, including fourteen killed, thirty-three wounded and twenty-one captured or missing. The Confederates lost five killed and twenty-six wounded and two pieces of artillery.[17]

The Rebel victory's effects were temporary as the fight at Scary Creek merely slowed Cox. With more Federal forces closing from the north and west, the Confederate commander, former Virginia governor Brigadier General Henry A. Wise, abandoned the Kanawha Valley and retreated 125 miles to Lewisburg.[18] In the Confederate retreat, Major Thomas L. Broun led a force of three hundred Rebel volunteers from Boone and Logan Counties up the Big Coal River through Boone and Raleigh Counties, southwest of Charleston, in the war's first large movement of military forces through the Coal River Valley region. Broun knew the land well since he recently had been the prewar president of the Coal River Navigation Company at Peytona, a post held before him by future Union army general William S. Rosecrans.[19]

Instead of stopping at Charleston, General Cox pursued the fleeing Confederates up the Kanawha Valley and marched his army thirty-eight miles directly to Gauley Bridge, entering the town on July 29. Cox's swift seizure of Gauley Bridge was one of the more significant early strategic achievements of the war in the mountains. The Federals' possession of Gauley Bridge, with its concentration of strategic lines of river and road communications throughout the region, significantly impeded Confederate resistance in south-central western Virginia. The Confederates were well aware that this force blocked their return to the Kanawha Valley and would need to be removed. Therefore, the forces of Brigadier Generals John B. Floyd and Wise engaged in numerous probing skirmishes in a wide arc to the south, southeast and northeast of Gauley Bridge, notably Big Sewell Mountain (August 16), Hawks Nest (August 20), Piggots Mill (August 25) and Kessler's Cross Lanes (August 26).

Meanwhile, violence and civil unrest intensified in the areas around the Kanawha Valley during the summer, especially in the Coal River Valley region, the rugged mountainous coal-rich lands astride the Big and Little Coal Rivers and their seemingly innumerable creeks and streams. Control of the Coal River region became an objective for both sides. The valley "was torn by internal strife between unionist and secessionist sympathizers. Although Raleigh County as a whole voted for secession, the Marsh and Clear Fork districts of the Coal River were strong Union sympathizers. Many neighbors and families were split, some sending soldiers to both the Union and Confederate armies."[20]

Coalsmouth (present-day St. Albans), at the confluence of the Coal and Kanawha Rivers in Kanawha County, became a major base for the Confederate army early in the war and afterward for the Union army. Before he retreated, "General Wise scuttled many barges of coal in an effort to block Union troop navigation up the Coal river and prevent the coal from ending up in Union hands."[21]

The adjacent countryside, however, swarmed with secessionists. The worst turmoil was in Boone County—named in honor of the famous pioneer Daniel Boone—where, throughout the summer in 1861, "the troops under Wise and the militia south of the river kept up a continual skirmishing."[22] On April 17, the county had passed the ordinance of secession, 317 to 226 in favor, and declared strongly for the Confederacy. Most county officials and "residents were on the side of the South."[23] The county's enlistment rate was two-thirds Confederate.[24] Rebel citizens and armed volunteers—characterized as "robbers and murderers" by the Northern press—harassed residents sympathetic to the Union.[25] In turn, armed Union volunteers—self-styled "Home Guards"—harassed residents sympathetic to the Confederacy. To defend against thieving and to protect their property, communities began organizing for self-defense.[26]

In great majority, the citizens were Confederate in sympathy; though there were in spots communities that held fast to their loyalty and allegiance to the old Union. It was these spots that were favorite targets for roving bands of Confederate partisans—for the most part irregulars who preyed upon the Federal loyalists and kept the entire area in a state of turmoil. There were reprisals and house burnings by the Unionists, which was held to be "rebellion" by the Confederate dissidents.[27]

The situation was only marginally less tenuous in the Clear Fork region, as the diary of a Coal River Valley resident attests:

The day before the election a neighbor of mine, who had professed all the time to be a Union man, came to me and told me that the Union was gone for certain and that we all had better vote for ratification and all secede

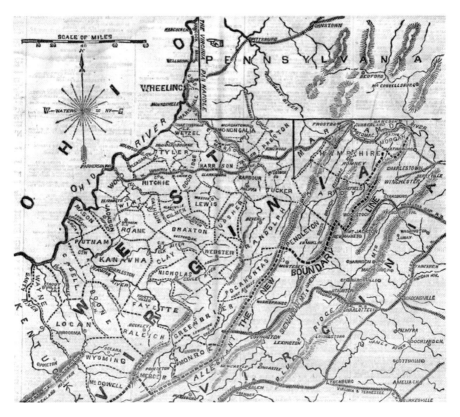

From the *New York Herald*, December 14, 1862.

together and show as bold a front as we could. He said that it would be better for us to divide the Union and set up a new government of our own and call it the Southern Confederacy. He also said his brother was a kind of a lawyer who lived at Raleigh Court House (Beckley) and had been down and explained the matter to him, and also told him that the colonel of the militia of our county would be down to our precinct at the election the next day, and would bring the sheriff and deputy sheriff of our county and armed forces to guard the polls. He said that all who voted for rejection of secession would forthwith be arrested and hanged. He also told me that they had a particular eye on me and if I voted a Union vote I would be certain to be killed…I soon found that all of the Union men would be compelled to keep their thoughts to themselves and not express them to no man, because the rebels had got to such a pitch that there were being quite a number of Union men shot and hanged. So I said as little as possible.[28]

The historical record does not reveal exactly when the Coal River Valley region first arose to Federal attention in the spring and summer of 1861. However, because of the increased danger of war between the North and South and the animated public debate about the West Virginia statehood movement, public meetings were held at largely pro-Union Peytona and pro-Confederate Boone Court House with resolutions calling on the people to prepare for war and steps taken to raise troops. The April 19 Virginia secession ballot was controlled by Confederate sympathizers who prevented the Union sympathizers from voting, and the Confederate flag was hoisted over the county courthouse on April 20 at a mass meeting at Boone Court House.

The state of affairs was comparable in the Clear Fork and Marsh Fork areas of the upper Coal River Valley in Raleigh County:

As the rebels got a few men together, they made great threats against the Union men and all who would not vote for the ratification of the Ordinance of Secession and canvassed every county, threatening to mob every man who spoke in favor of the Union, saying at the same time that they would establish a Southern Confederacy. They said that every man who voted for the Union was a black abolitionist and that as soon as they voted for the Union they would mob him, hang him and shoot him before he left the ground. By that means they kept a great many Union men from going to the polls.[29]

As Civil War historian Bruce Catton wrote of this early period of the war, "The border states appeared to be exploding like a string of firecrackers":

Against them was the power of a blazing sentiment, built on an old fondness and raised now by violence to story-book intensity. The bond that pulled American states into the Confederacy was always more a matter of emotion than of cold logic, and...the emotional response to the nineteenth of April was unrestrained. What the North saw as a mob scene looked in the South like a legendary uprising, with gallant heroes brutally done to death by the ignorant soldiers of a cruel despotism.[30]

Such "welling forth of sentiment" that attached itself to the Southern saga was rampant in southwestern Virginia, which largely felt kinship with the Old Dominion.

Meanwhile, General McClellan, in Union command of western Virginia, needed information about secessionist strength and movements and

Union spy Pryce Lewis (Pinkerton Detective Agency) performed intelligence gathering in the Kanawha Valley in the summer of 1861 for General McClellan. Lewis escaped the Confederate-controlled region via the Boone–Logan road to Chapmanville and then to Kentucky. *Library of Congress.*

relied on spies. He sent Union spy Pryce Lewis, an agent of the famed Pinkerton detective organization, to the region, which resulted in "one of the most spectacular feats of espionage in the early days of the war." After several weeks collecting intelligence, Lewis made his escape via the Coal River Valley along the Boone–Logan road.

At Brownstown (now Marmet) he turned to the south on a rough, rutted mountain road and, by hard driving, managed [via Peytona and Boone Court House, now Madison] *to reach Logan that day. There, it seemed he had jumped out of the frying pan into the fire; before they knew it, they were in the midst of an assembly of rebel troops, and again under strong suspicion.*

When questioned, Lewis claimed to be the son of an English cotton manufacturer; that he had been in the South to buy cotton and was now en route to Louisville to see the British Consul about getting his purchases released and shipped overseas. Col. Browning, commander of the Confederates, was called. Lewis turned on the charm and, with the aid of his last bottle of champagne, was able to convince the Colonel that he was an innocent English traveler and didn't know what all this pother was about.

In fact, Lewis made a hit with Browning, who pressed him to make a speech to his troops. And, on parting, dictated route memoranda directing the travelers to Pikeville, Kentucky, which they reached on the second day after leaving Logan. Then pressing on as fast as possible, Lewis and Bridgeman made their way into Catlettsburg, where their first sight was an American flag flying from a tall staff. For the first time they felt safe. Reaching Cincinnati a couple of days later, after an absence of nineteen days, Lewis made his report to Pinkerton, who immediately ordered him back to join Gen. Cox at Red House, on the Kanawha.[31]

Throughout the summer, then, hostile preparations and movements were underway everywhere. As Confederate troops began concentrating in the Kanawha Valley under General Wise at Charleston, Coal River Valley volunteers were organizing into companies to join the gray-clad forces. When Virginia seceded and the governor called out the state militia, the prewar 187th Virginia Militia Regiment (Boone) had been among the earliest to organize. About 475 men responded to the Confederate muster and began drilling.[32] About 350 of these ranks contributed companies primarily to the formation of the 22nd, 36th and 60th Virginia Infantry regiments; the 45th Virginia Infantry Battalion; the 8th Virginia Cavalry Regiment; and several other Virginia units.

The Boone militia belonged to Brigadier General Alfred A. Beckley's brigade, Wise's Legion, and formed a part of the Rebel army in the Kanawha Valley region. On June 25, 1861, Colonel Ezekiel S. Miller, commanding the 187th Regiment, reported two volunteer companies organized for service with Beckley's brigade. In calling up the militia under the laws of the state to muster, Miller warned the enrolled men of the militia that if any "did not rally to that call and did not obey the law he might expect as the penalty to be shot."[33] Almost all the Confederate and Union companies organizing were led by men who had been connected with the prewar county administration—for example, as sheriffs, justices of the peace, clerks, magistrates, assessors, surveyors, etc.

Several hundred Union men of Boone, however, generally refused to obey the call for the Virginia state militia to organize at Boone Court House. "Two militia companies, one on Mud River and the other at Peytona, where anti-secession sentiment was strong, refused to attend the muster."[34] As a result, Union militia were organizing for Federal service. These included Home Guard companies under Captains Cumberland Adkins (June 19), Cumberland Harless (June 19) and Jonathan Spurlock (July 10).[35]

There was a great deal of sympathy for the South, and the citizens did not want Federal troops in their midst. Union sentiment was strongest in the Peytona district along the Big Coal River, its Clear Fork region and the upper Pond Fork area of the Little Coal River, as well as smaller enclaves on Hewett Creek and Foster. In contrast, "finding Peytona men who were Confederate sympathizers was almost an impossibility."[36] The organization of pro-Union militia at Peytona, in particular, caused a sensation at Boone Court House and an outburst of anger among secessionists.

The 187th Regiment was called into field service at Boone Court House on August 15, when General Robert E. Lee, newly arrived in Confederate command in the western Virginia mountains, ordered Beckley's brigade (as the 35th Virginia Infantry Regiment) to join General Wise. Some of the 187th had already fought at Mud River Bridge (July 14) and Scary Creek (July 17). The first Rebel company to organize was Company A, which Miller himself commanded. The second was Company B, led by Captain Joel E. Stollings, clerk of the county court.[37] By late August, it was reported of Boone Court House that "a company of some 150 rebels entered the place a few days ago and took two U.S. officials prisoner."[38] Some 187th men were also in the Confederate ranks at Wayne Court House (August 26–27).[39]

Prewar animosities and antagonisms decisively contributed to the outbreak and ferocity of violence in the Coal River Valley region. Boone County was the center of gravity. Formed from parts of Kanawha, Cabell and Logan Counties in 1847, the southern part of Boone had come from Logan County, while the northern part came from Kanawha County. The Big Coal River, Rock Creek and Little Coal River below Rock Creek had been part of Kanawha County. (Only a small part, Mud River, had come from Cabell.) The object of creating the new county had been to exploit the region's vast natural resources of coal and timber.[40] This made it a fragile political union at the start.

Rock Creek, West Virginia, a frequent Coal River Valley thoroughfare for Union and Confederate forces. *Library of Congress.*

The question of where to locate the new county seat presented the first stumbling block. The rival communities were the Ballardsville area in the south, on the south bank of the Little Coal River, and Peytona in the north, on the north bank of the Big Coal River. After acrimonious debate, and in recognition of the sectional division of the new county, the representatives from north and south agreed to locate the county seat in the southern part of the county. Turtle Creek and Newport were considered before agreement was reached on Ballardsville. It was further agreed that the new state-funded public road planned from Brownstown (now Marmet) to Logan Court House would run through both the county seat and Peytona. In addition, the Big Coal region would get public improvements necessary to enable navigation by steamboats all the way to Peytona in order to send coal to Northern destinations.[41]

Consequently, throughout the 1840s and 1850s, the northern and southern parts of the new county gradually followed different paths, developing two different outlooks strangely similar to the rising schism separating the North and South of the larger United States itself. In the Peytona district (then stretching from present-day Peytona to Racine), the soil and mountainous terrain favored mostly smaller farmsteads in the northern part of the county rather than large

One of the facilities at Peytona built in connection with the first large-scale coal mining in the Coal River Valley, the "Old Stone Building" was a natural stop on the Boone–Logan road and was used as a mining commissary and offices. During the Civil War, it served as a meeting place, Union Home Guards post and a waypoint for Federal forces on their frequent raids in the area. The building stood until 1954, when it was destroyed by fire. *West Virginia Geological Survey (1915)*.

plantations, and by 1860, farming there was declining. Manned by immigrant labor from the northeast cities and Europe, industry was flourishing, fueled by mills, mining and road, rail and river transportation to haul the coal financed by a curious mixture of New York and Richmond investors.[42]

In contrast, agriculture remained the central feature of antebellum life along the Little Coal River. Fertile soil and the broader width of the Little Coal River Valley made it better suited for large-scale farms of cattle, sheep, hogs, tobacco, corn, wheat, apples, peaches, sugarcane (for molasses) and hay. While slaves were few in number overall in the county, most of them were concentrated along the Little Coal River in the Boone Court House area. And while the farming economy was beginning to stall throughout the county, mining in the north was experiencing a boom, and the economy was on an upswing. The geography and widening social, political and economic differences set Peytona and Boone Court House, in particular, at odds.

To further complicate matters, the rival communities continued to identify with and look primarily to their former mother counties where their family roots and kin were—the residents of the southern part of Boone with Logan clans, the northern part with Kanawha and the western part with Cabell- and Putnam-oriented clans. Boone Court House, in effect, became a place apart in imposing its political dominance. Peytona, after a decade of investment in industrial development—the Coal River system of locks and dams, rail, roads, mills and mining—was the center of a strong, growing body of militant Unionists and a curious outpost in the mountains of eastern finance, leavened by a significant free-labor immigrant element that abhorred slavery. The outbreak of the war gratified those in the Coal River Valley who were eager to drive out the secessionists with force of arms if necessary. For the even greater number of residents who sympathized with secession, the war was an expression of their fiercely guarded sense of themselves as free and independent people. Such was their contempt for the authority represented by the "Yankees."

For these combined reasons, conditions could not have been more conducive to exacerbating the political and economic rivalries. So when the war came, thus divided, the Coal River Valley was sure to see trouble. Boone County, in particular, enveloped in long-simmering and explosive animosity, very early got a wallop. Political organizing, residual antebellum hostilities and wartime developments emboldened first Peytona against Boone Court House. This provoked conditions in which a half dozen communities—Clear Fork, Marsh Fork, Pond Fork, Hewett Creek, Mud River and Foster—eventually aligned with Peytona, effectively enclosing Boone Court House.

By the summer of 1861, then, it had become clear that any peace in the region was little more than a truce that neither side strictly observed, as the war destroyed the bonds of common interests that, until now, had held the people together. The area was largely under Confederate control, and the Boone County Courthouse, for which the town was named, was being used as area headquarters. In contrast, the Peytona district was under pro-Union control, and a large stone building used as a commissary and offices for the Western Mining and Manufacturing Company served as a Union gathering place. Incidents of friction arose at once between Boone Court House and the more Union-leaning communities, especially Peytona and Pond Fork.

Union elements terrorized the families of the thousands of men in Wyoming, Raleigh and Boone Counties who had joined the Confederate army. In turn, Confederate elements terrorized Union people. In the mountains, the fathers and sons were typically the protectors and primary providers. When the men left home to fight, their families suffered terrible hardship lasting for years. Many women and children found themselves alone, running farms and businesses and defenseless against pitiless marauders. Roving this broad wilderness area, armed bands of each side stole horses and livestock, burned crops and plundered homesteads. They captured members of the other side and turned them over to authorities as prisoners of war. Unionists were shot or hanged, especially in Raleigh County.

Throughout the war years in the Coal River Valley, "both sides raided anywhere they could. If somebody was a sympathizer with the other side, they took what they had and almost starved them to death. These people moved on top of the mountains to get away from people finding them…they were afraid and that was the only way they could escape because somebody would come along and just kill them."[43]

As the rumors and actual incidents of civil violence increased, and after hearing of the terrorist acts from their families, the men who had left the region as volunteers for the Confederate army asked for leave to return and protect their homes. It was not unusual for men to go home with or without permission. Therefore, being listed as deserted did not always mean that a soldier had actually deserted in the strict military sense. Sometimes the soldier joined another unit, became wounded and was left behind or went home to visit family or to protect them.

The date is not known, but in an action on the Big Coal River at Coon's Mill (present-day Seth)—possibly in August 1861—a detachment of "13 Rebel Rangers home on leave, it is claimed, routed 150 home guards from Kanawha county."[44] Most likely, the Confederate soldiers were from the Boone Rangers, a company of Big Coal volunteers raised by Captain James W. McSherry, of Peytona, for service with the Thirty-sixth Virginia Infantry Regiment, and the Twenty-second Virginia Infantry Regiment's Companies I and K, which were raised in whole or in part in Boone County. The companies fought at Scary Creek in July and afterward retreated from the Kanawha Valley toward Lewisburg with Major Broun via the Big Coal River Valley.

The mountainous region lent itself to agriculture in the valleys and in the rare small expanse of flat land found in hollows, passes and gaps in the mountain chains. Therefore, the attachment of the people to their farms usually of only a few acres was intense. From the ground, they drew both their living and the balances on which depended not only their families' survival during the hard mountain winters but also their status as free and independent people. The consequences of any threat to invade his fields, destroy his orchards or burn his crops—a recurrent theme of the violent mountain warfare that had been waged by the pioneers and Indians—greatly contributes to explaining the ferocity of the inter-communal fighting that occurred in the western Virginia mountains when the Civil War broke out, especially in the Coal River Valley.[45]

Therefore, because hearth and field were left vulnerable when they marched off to war, the volunteers placed the highest premium on settling matters head on and as quickly as possible. In this way, many troops, Union and Confederate alike, volunteered only to protect the Kanawha Valley. Many Rebels, fleeing past their homes in Broun's retreat, were concerned for their families and left their units with or without permission to defend their homes. The Twenty-second and Thirty-sixth Virginia Regiments were particularly affected by such "desertions" as, in some cases, entire companies disappeared to protect their families and farms.[46] The Union men who were humiliated in the fight at Coon's Mill were likely the Peytona Home Guards. Coon's Mill was possibly the action in which Confederate private Fenell Morris, Company I, Twenty-second Virginia Infantry, was shot and killed in Big Coal country in August 1861.[47]

In an affair on the Spruce Fork of the Little Coal River, a group of men from the Clear Fork of the Big Coal in Raleigh County and their local Boone acquaintances suspected of organizing for Federal purposes were surrounded by three dozen Rebel militia, who rushed up to the house where they were staying and arrested them at dawn. Taken to Boone Court House, they were put through questioning and a mock trial before Colonel Miller, who was staunchly pro-secessionist in his sympathies. In addition to commanding the Boone militia, Miller was also the county magistrate, and in the crisis he saw it as his duty to uphold the Old Dominion, arresting and jailing citizens deemed traitorous. The leader of the Union men, William S. Dunbar, wrote in his diary:

Just after daylight, I stepped out into the yard and saw that we were surrounded by armed men who rushed up to the house...we were abused by almost all of them. They searched all of us, even to our pocket books and little papers and accounts we had. They found my class book with the several preachers' names in it whom they said they were acquainted with.

They looked over the book and names, and as they came to the elders' and circuit riders' names they would curse them with the most bitter oaths, and say they would hang everyone of them if they could get hold of them, calling all of them damned abolitionists. When they came to my name as the leader they turned to me and swore revenge, saying that I was a damned black abolitionist and was the captain of a band of conspirators and that the men who were with me were a part of the band and that they would hang us all.

After keeping us there a considerable time under their abuse, one of the Barretts went off with my class book and said he was going to burn the damned abolition paper and get shut of it that much. I never saw it any more and never heard what became of it. I suppose it was burned.

They kept us there all day and went through a time of mock trials before Ezekiel Miller, who was their colonel and a magistrate…They also tried to pick flaws in us by asking us questions separate from each other. They questioned me first. After they found that they could not catch me by my own talk they called in all the rest of the men, one at a time, and questioned them very closely, especially me.

I soon saw that the whole thing was aimed at me in order to condemn me and have some fun as they collected information, and then hang or shoot me, but they failed in every attempt and finally got ashamed of themselves and released us all. However, they made all the rest of the men who were with us go back home except me and my two brothers-in-law…We went on to our journey's end and when we got ready we went home, which was about a week after that.[48]

In another incident, a Confederate guerrilla band seeking arms raided Bald Knob, located along the border separating Boone and Wyoming Counties. They seized the U.S. post office and tied the postmaster, Jasper Workman, and his brother William Jesse Workman together for a day and a night while they looted the office and rested.[49]

Fervent Union supporter Samuel Scragg, a Welsh immigrant and civil engineer, was supervisor at the Peytona Mines, among the earliest commercial coal mining operations in the region.

After a considerable amount of talking and urging people to support the government at Washington, he was arrested or rather captured by the Home Guards of the Confederacy, stationed at the county seat. He was in the custody of a man by the name of Dolan, expecting to be prescribed and summarily shot when Dolan volunteered to let him escape.

He said to Mr. Scraggs [sic]: "I know the lines and the pass words. I can get you through the lines. If you will go to Charleston, traveling through the woods, the Union forces will protect you." Mr. Scraggs [sic] said, "I accepted the invitation. When I reached the camp on the south side of the Kanawha, I told my story to the Colonel."[50]

Circuit-riding Methodist minister Robert Hager, "from Six Mile on Spruce Fork and an ardent supporter of freedom," was one of the larger landowners south of the Kanawha River and strongly opposed secession.[51]

> *Being active, and exercising a good deal of influence he became especially obnoxious to the secessionists and the day before the May election he was arrested for "treason to the State." He made his escape and fled to Ohio...Then they began to rob his family and farm of everything they could carry away and use, and waylaying and shooting at members of his family.*[52]

Later, as a member of the West Virginia statehood movement, Hager "told the members of the Wheeling Convention that the Union Men in Boone County did not have the courage to vote for secession because of threats and in fear of a drunken secession mob at the Court House."[53]

Meanwhile, at the public meetings of citizens held at Peytona, Union sympathizers denounced the Confederacy and formed the Peytona Home Guards militia company. They were armed with "about 80 muskets obtained by means of Col. [Lewis] Ruffner, in Charleston, Kanawha County, being the thrown away guns, at the time Henry A. Wise retreated from Charleston."[54] Union men on the Pond and Clear Forks also began organizing. The Peytona, Clear Fork and Pond Fork companies provided troops who helped form the Eighth (West) Virginia Infantry Regiment. Mounted as the famed Seventh (West) Virginia Cavalry later in the war, the regiment was active in the pursuit of Stonewall Jackson up the Shenandoah Valley; Pope's Northern Virginia campaign; Averell, Crook and Hunter's great raids; and the Battles of Droop Mountain, Rocky Gap and Cloyd's Mountain.[55]

The Pond Fork Home Guards militia obstructed key roads to control several important "mountain passes at the head of Coal River."[56] Near Walnut Gap, they built a mountainside fort of entrenchments and breastworks of timber and rocks along the Skin Fork stretch of the Little Coal's Pond Fork for their protection. Active on the Pond Fork, they captured and paroled two Rebel militia scouts (Privates Morris Cook and Henry Clay) and threatened to invade Wyoming County and burn the town of Wyoming Court House (Oceana). One of the captured Rebel scouts professed to be a Union man and learned that the Home Guards expected the arrival of a regiment of Union troops and that one of the Home Guards' leaders, Private William Workman, had gone after them.[57]

The idea of Union soldiers entering the region, bent on maltreatment of the South, stung the sensitivities of the Coal River Valley's numerous

Southern sympathizers. The recruitment and organizing of Federal militia in their midst at Peytona, Clear Fork and Pond Fork set the backwoods settlements of the Coal River Valley ablaze with fear and anticipation.[58] A resident of the region wrote in his diary that the entire area

> *was then in a great excitement and the cry of "the Yankees are coming" was heard from every quarter. All the South was scared terribly. They thought the Yankees were a dreadful set of fellows, having heard that the Union Army was sweeping everything before them, killing men, women and children. They were hiding and running in every direction, moving their property off to Dixie.*[59]

As trouble began to occur with acts of hostility and violence, Unionists and Southerners alike were organizing and fortifying positions. Many, such as Dr. George A. Vandelinde, one of the county's few physicians and sympathetic to the Confederacy, moved their families deeper into the mountains to escape the marauders who roamed the country stealing horses, cattle and crops and committing murders.[60] Where Vandelinde lived, at lower Rock Creek, about three and a half miles north of Boone Court House, a mixture of allegiances prevailed. From the Netherlands, Vandelinde was forty-eight years old and had served in the Belgian Revolution (1830–32). During the Civil War, he provided medical services to both Federal and Confederate soldiers equally after battles and while they convalesced at home on furloughs.[61]

Dr. George A. Vandelinde, of Rock Creek, Boone County, surgeon, 187th (Boone) Regiment of Virginia state militia. *Author's collection.*

Because of the departure of so many men serving in the Confederate army, the numbers of Union and Confederate militia in the county roughly evened. The change in the balance of power hastened Colonel Miller, who imagined himself beset by growing hostile forces, to deter the internal revolt. The Southern sympathizers established their regimental headquarters ("Camp Boone") on August 27 at Boone Court House, thirty-eight miles from Charleston. Miller called for the militia loyal to Virginia to concentrate there. So here was Miller, in command of the Rebel force at Boone Court House, confronting his former fellow county official Joseph H. Barker, whose pro-Union militia company garrisoned Peytona. Miller sent General Wise urgent word that a Federal attack was expected and, therefore, to rush reinforcements to him at Boone Court House.[62]

Meanwhile, the rumors of escalating violence reached Charleston. Union men such as Scragg and Workman were bringing General Cox news of the Rebels organizing at Boone Court House. In addition to Scragg, the two Union militia men the Rebels had captured, including Captain Cumberland Harless, were being held in the county jail at Boone Court House.[63] Causing even greater terror among the citizens were the bushwhackers, marauders and horse thieves who preyed on isolated homesteads. Men on both sides, as well as men who did not belong to either army, were stealing horses and livestock in the name of "the army" and taking them for their own use.[64] All of this was as clear to General Cox as it needed to be. Something had to be done, and so the initiative came from the Federal army, as the conditions brought on a crisis larger than the ambitious Boone Confederates had bargained for.

Monitoring the hostility of the Rebel volunteers south of the Kanawha River, General Cox rapidly got things underway. He organized an expedition into the Coal River Valley.[65] The arrest of Captain Harless "was thought to be the immediate cause," as the Peytona Home Guards, on hearing of his confinement, dispatched a messenger, Second Lieutenant William Gramm, to the Federal army for assistance.[66] On August 27, Companies A and D of the Twenty-sixth Ohio Infantry Regiment were sent on a reconnaissance mission up the Coal River toward Boone Court House. They returned the next day with two Rebel prisoners after marching to the "Forks of Coal" (Alum Creek) and back, thirty-four miles. The scouting foray established that a Rebel militia force indeed was organizing at Boone Court House.[67] The town was strategically located at the center of the road network of the Little Coal River and its main branches, the Pond and Spruce Forks; the Boone–Logan road; and the Pond Fork road to Wyoming and Raleigh Counties.

In the meantime, in the ongoing struggle for Gauley Bridge in the New River country, General Cox advanced his pickets south toward Fayette Court House (Fayetteville). Confederate cavalry, scouting toward Kanawha Falls four miles below Gauley Bridge, drove in the Federal pickets at Cotton

Hill. Supplying his forces operating deep in the mountains was already proving to be a logistical challenge. As Cox moved eastward, the difficulties to maintain a workable line of supply increased. A general who realized the importance of supplies in the mountains, Cox established his main depot at Charleston and posts at Camp Piatt (Belle) and Brownstown (Marmet). The Confederate cavalry action at Gauley Bridge revealed the exposed position of Cox's army if an enemy force managed to take Cotton Hill. As the Kanawha Valley's population was roughly split in loyalties between North and South and many communities were divided, Cox was reminded frequently that the Confederates in his rear were not far distant.

The reports of Union scouts reaching Cox estimated the Confederate force at Boone Court House to be at least four hundred to six hundred men. With such confirmation, Cox gradually was able to catch on to what was happening south of the Kanawha. The Union general concluded, as he put it, that the gathering threatened "to menace our communications with the Ohio."[68] From the reports, it was feared that the Rebel force would be one thousand strong within a few days.[69] Cox could not remain quiescent; conditions at Gauley Bridge were too precarious. He was therefore compelled by the pressure of events and increasing concern for the stability of his long, tenuous supply line and the security of the Federal rear to do something. In order to restore order in his rear and south of the Kanawha, as well as to free the Federal prisoners held at Boone Court House and support the Union militia who were organizing companies in the Coal River Valley, Cox believed he knew what to do and acted vigorously.[70]

On August 29, the Union general ordered a force assembled at Charleston to deal with the growing threat south of the Kanawha River. The speed and manner in which the Federals undertook the operation, as General Cox said, to "beat up" the Rebels suggested the imminent threat that the Union army perceived.[71] In accordance with the goal of securing Gauley Bridge, then, the Federals swept into the Coal River Valley with the purpose of crushing Confederate resistance and weakening the will of the people of Boone, in particular, to support the Confederacy. Rapid measures were taken for what became the most famous event in the Coal River Valley during the Civil War, remembered a century and half afterward in the annals of the great fratricidal conflict as the Battle of Boone Court House or, sometimes alternatively, the Battle of Boone County Courthouse.

Chapter 2

BOONE COURT HOUSE

In 1861, Boone Court House, Virginia, was a village on the southern bank of the Little Coal River and the county seat of Boone County. Also called Boone, Boonetown, Booneville, Boonesville and Ballardsville, the village was situated in a gorge carved by the action of the Pond Fork and Spruce Fork Rivers, which merge at the town to form the Little Coal River. The town consisted of the courthouse, the county jail, a post office, a school, churches, a mill, businesses and houses arrayed around a two-acre public square, with a population of about 150. In addition to fertile soil for agriculture along the rivers, the area was a source for the manufacture of wooden barges that hauled coal on the Coal and Kanawha Rivers.[72]

About 240 miles (in a direct line) west of Richmond, the village occupied a broad alluvial outcrop of level bottomland for one thousand feet west of where the two forks met. Surrounding forested mountains dominated the place. Overlooking the area a half mile immediately north of the village was Knob Hill, an eight-hundred-foot round top (present-day Reservoir Hill in Madison); to the east Miller Hill; and to the west and south the Little Coal ridge of Piney Knob. During the following years until the war ended, the town changed hands numerous times, often without official record, as forces of both North and South passed through and preyed on the population throughout the area.

No stranger to war, the place had been the site of a wilderness battle between frontiersman and Indians in August 1785. Following a Shawnee massacre of settlers on the Bluestone Creek, a branch of the New River in Mercer County, settlers pursued the Indians and overtook a portion of their raiding party near the mouth of the Pond Fork River. In the battle that followed at a bottom on the west bank of the Pond Fork, about a half mile above its junction with the Spruce Fork of the Little Coal River (along the current Old River Road, County Highway 79/03), many Indians fell to the fire of the pursuers.[73]

To organize the Federal expedition in the late summer of 1861, General Cox selected Colonel James V. Guthrie, who commanded the First Kentucky Infantry Regiment.[74] Guthrie, who was also serving as the Union garrison commander at Charleston at this time, assigned to the operation the following units that were available to him from Cox's Kanawha Brigade, West Virginia, Department of the Ohio:

First Kentucky: Company A (Captain Joseph T. Wheeler)
Fourth (West) Virginia Infantry: Companies B (Captain John L. Vance) and
  D (Captain Arza M. Goodspeed)
Twenty-sixth Ohio Infantry: Companies G (Captain Samuel C. Rook) and
  K (Captain William H. Squires)
First Kentucky Light Artillery: Simmonds' Battery, also called the Twenty-third
  Independent Battery, Ohio Light Artillery (Captain Seth J. Simmonds)[75]

Realizing that marching on foot would not get the Federal troops to Boone Court House in time, Guthrie embarked the force aboard several paddle-wheel steamboats at Charleston, including the Kanawha River flotilla's flagship, the army gunboat *Silver Lake No. 2*. The transports slipped their cables and proceeded up the Kanawha River on August 29. The boats steamed ten miles and made shore at the landing at Brownstown (present-day Marmet), about fifteen miles northeast of Peytona, the Big Coal River steamboat landing about sixteen miles northeast of Boone Court House.[76] Thus, in this cooperative effort of the Union army and naval forces, the troops covered a quarter of the eighty-two-mile round trip they traveled afloat.

It was a good plan, and Guthrie moved swiftly as ordered. He first sent forth two companies. Company G, Twenty-sixth Ohio Infantry Regiment, was called the "Carroll Guards" and was from the Mahoning County area in Ohio and named after the mayor of Youngstown, Reuben Carroll. The soldiers of Company A, First Kentucky Infantry Regiment, were from the Louisville area. The Federal force was guided from Brownstown by the prewar Peytona Mining Company foreman, Samuel Scragg, who had escaped from Confederate imprisonment at Boone Court House and reported his experience at Charleston.[77]

The army gunboat *Silver Lake No. 2* served as flagship for the flotilla of steamboats that supported the Boone Court House expedition. A 129-ton, six-gun steam packet, it patrolled and operated as a transport in 1861–62 from Point Pleasant as far up as Brownstown (present-day Marmet), the head of steamboat navigation on the Kanawha River. *Taken from* Photographic History of the Civil War: The Navies *(1911)*.

On the following day, August 30, Guthrie dispatched Company K, Twenty-sixth Ohio Infantry Regiment, to reinforce the first two companies.[78] These troops were known as the "Cowling Videttes," named after a leading citizen involved in their formation in Madison County, Ohio, where they were raised. To cover Peytona and his line of communications with the Kanawha, and to threaten a Federal advance toward Raleigh Court House (present-day Beckley), the Fourth (West) Virginia companies followed as an ample reserve "that the two companies might fall back upon it, if they found the enemy too strong."[79] Together, these Federal companies made the march southward from Brownstown over the mountains and through deep ravines along Lens Creek to Mouth of Short Creek (present-day Racine), about eleven miles from Brownstown.

Private Timothy H. Deasy, Company G, Twenty-sixth Ohio Infantry, wrote:

> *We left Charleston about the last of August 1861 and went up Loop Creek on the banks of the Kanawha River. Loop Creek is on the far side of the*

Union private Timothy H. Deasy, Company G, Twenty-sixth Ohio Infantry Regiment, fought at Boone Court House. He authored the only known eyewitness report with details of the Union battle plan. *From the* Cleveland Press, *May 1949.*

river from Charleston, W.Va. We waded across Loop Creek I don't know how many times that night and were wet to our necks the next morning not from the depth of the water but from falling on the slippery stones.[80]

Until the blue column reached Mouth of Short Creek, the Confederates would be unable to determine whether the invaders were making for the Coal River Road to threaten Raleigh Court House from the north or for the Boone–Logan road and headed southward for Boone Court House. When the force reached Mouth of Short Creek, however, they took the southwesterly fork toward Peytona. The strategic suspense lifted, as it no longer was possible to hide their destination, and there was no longer any question about what Enyart's objective was. The Union march became an open movement directed at Boone Court House by way of Drawdy Creek, Rock Creek, across Newport Mountain, to the plains of Little Coal and then up the Little Coal River. The Fourth (West) Virginia Infantry companies seemingly remained at Peytona, scouting the Big Coal country toward Raleigh County and guarding the Federal rear and route of retreat as a blocking force, should the expedition to Boone Court House go awry.

Meanwhile, Colonel Miller lay at Camp Boone at Boone Court House assembling his Confederate force. It consisted of about 150 men organized into two companies of the Boone Rebel militia. Southern supporters observed the Federal soldiers as they left Charleston aboard steamers and were carried up the Kanawha River to the steamboat landing at Brownstown. This resourceful act was reported to Miller by his scouts. In this way, the Confederates were forewarned that the Federals were moving a force southward, with an appearance of haste to smite the gathering of Southern militia at Boone Court House. Colonel Miller therefore expected to be attacked at any time. To protect the county seat, the center of Confederate authority over the region, was the immediate concern of the Rebels.[81]

Born in Monroe County in 1813, Colonel Ezekiel Miller was forty-eight years old when the Civil War broke out. He was the son of John Miller, a veteran of the War of 1812 who had been a colonel in the Virginia militia (Monroe). Ezekiel Miller's grandfather had been a Hessian soldier in the American Revolution who deserted his command and joined the colonial forces. When Boone County was formed from parts of Logan, Kanawha and Cabell Counties, Ezekiel Miller was selected to serve among the county commissioners. He was later elected county magistrate and, as justice of the peace, organized the Boone militia. His views favored states' rights, and he was generally looked upon as a spokesman for secession and the county's most militarily knowledgeable official. He did not own slaves.

Despite his patriotic ardor, Miller was doubtful he could hold Boone Court House against the numbers confronting him. He appealed for assistance from the neighboring counties sympathetic to the South. The men of Logan, the mother county to most of the men at Boone Court House, lost no time responding to the appeal. By August 30, elements of the 129th Virginia Militia Regiment (Logan) began arriving, as Miller pronounced, to help repel "the invasion of Federal troops, and to put down the rebellion among the disloyal citizens of Boone, against the laws of the State and the Confederate States of America."[82] The influx of reinforcements, notably men of the Black Striped Company, an irregular band that operated in the country between the Guyandotte, Mud and Coal Rivers, increased the Confederate strength at Boone Court House to about 225 men in all. The broad bottomlands south of the town became a military campground.[83]

Reinforcement of the Confederate gathering at Boone Court House was exactly what General Cox had been worrying about. The Rebel militia belonged to various companies. Some were armed citizens who did not belong to the organized militia at all and were led by officers who had not been formally commissioned (a condition also true of the Union militia). The Rebel militia were patriotic for the South, but poorly equipped, practically unarmed and lacking uniforms, their determination to resist the Union invasion would prove unequal in the crucible.

Their ranks included Virginia state senator William D. Pate, brother of the famed pro-slavery advocate and Confederate cavalry leader Captain Henry Clay Pate.[84] The Pate clan was prominent in Boone County, where Pate's widowed mother and two brothers lived at Mouth of Short Creek. William Pate and his late father had founded the prewar Coal River Navigation Company, which established the locks and dams on the Big Coal and Little Coal Rivers. Another younger brother, Edmund, was an Episcopal priest. All three brothers were Confederate officers, and William Pate's political stumping for the Old Dominion contributed to the rising tensions in the Coal River Valley.

In addition, an interesting historical theory generally entertained is that the reinforcements from Logan County might also have included Confederate militia private William A. "Devil Anse" Hatfield, later famous as the leader of the Hatfield-McCoy feud.[85] "Devil Anse" Hatfield, the patriarch of his namesake clan, is often identified with the 129th Virginia Militia and its sister regiment, the 187th. Both regiments included many of Hatfield's family, friends and neighbors, and he is often associated with these units' service in the summer and autumn of 1861.[86]

The 550 Federals camped Friday night, August 30, at Peytona. The following day, the force advanced to the plains of Little Coal at Red House (also known then as Newport, presently Danville on West Virginia State Route 85), within two miles of its goal. Meanwhile, there was growing unrest and anticipation among the Confederate troops at Boone Court House. They wanted to fight and march on Peytona and push the Federals back to

The Hatfield family. Confederate soldier (and later captain) William A. "Devil Anse" Hatfield (second row, second from left), later of Hatfield-McCoy feud fame, fought at Boone Court House, according to oral tradition. *West Virginia State Archives.*

Brownstown. They knew they were outnumbered, but faced with a decision of attack, wait to be attacked or withdraw, Colonel Miller determined to loose his small force on the Federals when they emerged from the mountains.

The Confederate advance elements came out and boldly attacked the Federals at Red House on Saturday, August 31. The Union guide Scragg reported: "When we arrived at the camp at Danville [Red House] we encountered Home Guard Scouts, and a battle ensued."[87] Richmond's *Times Dispatch* newspaper, citing Virginia state senator William Pate's report, lauded the Confederate assault, which, although valiant and bravely executed, was severely defeated. Thus the Battle of Boone Court House began with a spirited encounter at Red House as the Rebels attacked and were repulsed after a twenty-minute fight. The *Times Dispatch* reported "the fight a desperate one." The Twenty-sixth Ohio Regiment's field and staff report called it "a sharp encounter."[88] One Confederate was killed, two wounded, six captured and several horses shot and rifles lost.[89] As the Union report does not mention casualties, it is possible that in this fight, the Federals lost none.

Afterward, "very bloody and bearing their wounded with them," the Rebels retreated back to Boone Court House. Their return "produced a very great excitement in the village," whose residents had not yet realized the terrible destruction awaiting them.[90] The Federal force lay on their arms that night at Red House, anxiously anticipating the next day's battle.[91] In contrast, the smaller Confederate force waited in its place on the alluvial plain at the confluence of the Spruce and Pond Forks of Little Coal, where the advance guard of the Union army found the Rebels the next day.

September 1 was a Sunday. The Federal force marched out of its camp at Red House early in the morning and advanced the two miles to Boone Court House along the Boone–Logan road. They had been joined by 200 local Union militia. These were the Home Guard men from Peytona, Pond Fork and Mud River for the most part, and likely some Wyoming Home Guards. In anticipation of an attack by the Union army from Charleston, which had been expected for some time, the Peytona men were organized as Company I, Eighth (West) Virginia Infantry Regiment. The Pond Fork men enlisted as Company B, Eighth (West) Virginia Infantry. This was the modest beginning of the famed Union regiment in which over 1,700 men eventually served during the war. The militia reinforcements increased the Federal ranks to 750 men. It was Colonel Miller's last chance to escape with his command before the Federals landed another blow, yet he did not take it.

Few people knew what to expect when the fighting broke out. For weeks, the rhetoric had been more heated than the events in the field. However, after the frenzied retreat of the Confederate force from the plains of Little Coal, the conflict took a disastrous turn for the Confederates troops and citizens. It became clear that the little village of Boone Court House now was the focus of the first significant Union army action of the war in the valley. Realizing the danger, the town's civilians fled the scene in an effort to avoid the coming violence. They made their way up Piney Knob and Miller Hill and watched the battle from the mountainsides.[92]

Colonel Enyart instructed the Union militia to advance toward Boone Court House in order to feel out the front without bringing on a general engagement. Thus, the Union plan of attack entailed, in effect, a demonstration or reconnaissance in force by the Union militia. The militia had no overall commander, so Corporal James W. Nowlin (Nowlen), First Kentucky Infantry Regiment (Company A), was put in charge of their movement.[93] Enyart instructed Nowlin to advance up the Boone–Logan road to draw the enemy's fire. When the Southern fire had been fixed, the Union militia would fall back on the main Union body. Enyart would then try to turn his enemy's right flank by fording the Little Coal River across to the mouth of Spruce, which he determined was the best place to attack the Rebel position. Both groups of Federals used "a handful of Peytona men as their guides."[94]

The position held by the Confederates was a weak one. It consisted of the town separated from the Federals by the Little Coal River but dominated by the eight-hundred-foot round top Knob Hill, overlooking the area a half mile immediately north of the village. At once, the Federals recognized the commanding height to be the key to the battlefield. Colonel Enyart selected Captain Wheeler with three infantry companies, one of the First Kentucky and two of the Twenty-sixth Ohio, and two of Simmonds' guns for the job. Thus, the hill was occupied by the Federal force in strength and guns posted. Outnumbered, poorly armed in comparison to their Federal counterparts and without supplies or artillery of their own to counter the enemy's strength, the Rebel position was untenable. However, although they had lost a number of men already, the Confederates did not want to evacuate the town and withdraw without another show of fight.

In this way, it came about that, according to the report of Private Deasy, Twenty-sixth Ohio Infantry Regiment (Company G), the Union militia

Little Coal River north of present-day Madison, about fifty years after the Civil War. In the left center foreground can be seen the commanding heights of Knob Hill, which figured prominently in the Battle of Boone Court House on September 1, 1861. *West Virginia Geological Survey (1915).*

Union artillery in action. Simmonds' Battery was cited for being "thoroughly reliable" and performing "good service" through all of the autumn 1861 campaign in the Kanawha and Coal River Valleys. *Taken from* Battles and Leaders of the Civil War *(1888)*.

companies defiantly advanced according to the plan of attack. The militia "part of our command marched down the public road to attract the attention of the rebels."[95] They advanced far enough to stimulate a forceful response from the Confederates. The Rebels complied with their role as Enyart expected and pushed their ranks to the south bank of the Little Coal River and commenced firing at the enemy. A Confederate flag flew defiantly over the Boone County Courthouse. The Federals saw a solid wall of men in gray, butternut and homespun, their muskets, shotguns and rifles blazing not one hundred yards away across the river.

However, when the Union militia had drawn the Confederate fire and the time came for them to fall back, they did not obey. They would not fall back. As the *Gallipolis Journal* reported, the militia refused to "budge an inch in that direction. They had had so many indignities heaped upon them by the overbearing Secessionists, when they had not the power to resent them, and now, having an opportunity to settle old scores, they were not inclined to let a chance slip."[96]

The Union men stood bravely and returned fire as a hot engagement took place in which the rival militias traded fire—the Federals from the river's north shore, the Confederates from the south. The two lines stood for about half an hour and fired away at each other as fast as they could reload. The firing, noise and smoke were appalling. Men on both shores of the river fell, while others kept on firing. The dense smoke settled down upon the valley so that after the initial volleys it became difficult to see effectively in any direction.

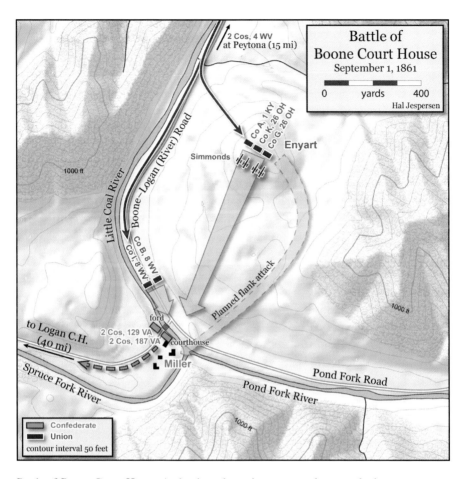

Battle of Boone Court House. At the time, the action was noted among the important battles and strategic moments thus far in the war. *Author's collection.*

Nearly 1,000 troops then were engaged in the battle—750 Federals and Union militia against 225 Confederate militia. The war in western Virginia was extremely difficult on families, and the Coal River Valley was a sterling microcosm. At Boone Court House, symbolic of the divided nation, brothers were pitted against one another, fathers against sons and cousins and in-laws against one another on the same battlefield. Families interrelated through marriage split in their loyalties, and the impact lasted for generations. There were countless greater battles during the Civil War than the skirmish at Boone Court House but few where two lines of blue and gray family and neighbors stood so close together and coldly fired into each other's ranks with such fierce determination.

The little log courthouse, standing atop a small rise above the river where floods could not reach it, anchored the Confederate front, which extended on both sides of the Boone–Logan road. It was Colonel Enyart's purpose to have Nowlin keep the Rebels occupied in the vicinity of the ford while he mounted a flank attack. However, the intensity of the fire and infernal din of the troops on both sides, standing against those lines of fire for those awful thirty minutes, stirred the First Kentucky's Captain Wheeler (Company A) to improvisation. Fretting on the hill, and as the battle grew more severe, he could restrain himself no longer. The plan of flanking the Rebels frustrated, he sounded the advance. It would seem that the Federal companies were lying against the hill close up to the summit, for the Rebels were astonished when the ranks of blue-clad soldiers "went down over the hill on the double quick."[97] They charged down the hill "like an avalanche," according to Private Deasy. Captain Rook, a Mexican War veteran who had landed at Vera Cruz with Winfield Scott, was at their head. Captain Wheeler—praised afterward as "gallant" and "brilliant" for directing the charge—became one of the war's early Union heroes.[98]

Some of the Rebels fled "Rook's Charge," but the main body stood firm and responded with spirit. Their firing was rapid and terrific, but the onrushing Federals did not stop. They plunged into the Little Coal and began to ford the river while under fire. "Part of the troops entered along the waterways while the remainder came through the hills."[99] The Union troops, along with the Home Guards, "attacked and drove the Confederate militia back into the town where they took defensive positions."[100] The Rebels briefly resisted and withstood the attack until the Federals were across the river.[101] The Rebel militia, defending their county and homes, held their ground in the path of the oncoming Federals until they began giving way under the weight of numbers.

Then occurred the crisis of the day. The Confederates, who had stood up unflinchingly under the strain despite their disadvantages, found the intense fire meted out by small arms at close range too much to bear. Believing that they faced 1,200 Federals charging, the Rebels broke and began withdrawing up the Spruce Fork road.[102] They turned and fled, and in a few minutes, a disorderly stream was pouring down the road past the town. Those who had not been shot were running for safety—200 of them. The Rebels "at once took to their heels, and such tall running as was done by those F.F.Vs., has never been seen since the race between Gildersleeve and the American Deer," according to an observer's report.[103]

Captain Samuel C. Rook, commander, Company C, Twenty-sixth Ohio Infantry Regiment. Rook's Charge broke the Confederate defense at Boone Court House. *Courtesy of descendant Edith Patsko.*

The Federals who stormed ashore carried the south bank of the river on the heels of the Confederate withdrawal. Into the gap thus created, without pausing, swarmed the triumphant Federals, led by the intrepid Captain Rook. Displacing the fleeing Rebels from the plain, they poured in like a torrent "and cleaned out the town in a little while."[104] The Federals charged down the road in pursuit of the flying enemy, collecting prisoners. At first, the troops encountered no resistance as they moved quickly through the town to prevent trouble after the Rebels fled. But Boone Court House was known as a rough and unruly place, and in the Union view, treason there was rife. Not surprisingly, the Federals found some residents still spoiling for a fight.

As Private Samuel G. Birch, a twenty-eight-year-old color-bearer of the Twenty-sixth Ohio Infantry Regiment, marched through the town, he flouted the American flag.[105] A shot rang out from an unknown source. Birch fell, having been shot through both hips. The fate of the shooter is unknown, but local tradition holds that Birch was shot by a withdrawing Rebel or a resident who was then himself fatally shot by the Federals, or that the identity of the resident was not discovered. One tradition remembered—with a ring of embellishment impossible to judge, after all this time—is that "Devil Anse" Hatfield fired the fateful shot that felled Birch. Another tradition is that a wealthy plantation owner and slaveholder pulled the trigger.[106]

If the latter were so, several local candidates fit the stereotype. They included Henry H. Hopkins, whose large slaveholding family was regarded as "one of the old and honored ones of the South."[107] He was known to the Union army "as a notorious Secessionist living near Coal River" and was "personally engaged in the combat at Boone C.H."[108] William

Smoot, also of an old and prominent family in Virginia, a compatriot of Hopkins and member of another of the largest slave-owning families, was among the numerous citizens of Confederate sentiment captured at Boone Court House and taken as prisoners to Charleston.[109] Kept in wretched conditions, their captivity during the fall was a harrowing ordeal from which some never returned.

St. Clair Ballard, after whom Ballardsville was named, was another ardent secessionist and the patriarch of a large slaveholding family. His lands below Boone Court House served as the site of Camp Boone, the Confederate encampment. The idea of naming the new county after Daniel Boone had been Ballard's as a member of the Virginia legislature in 1847.[110] (As a child, Ballard's mother had been rescued from Indians by Daniel Boone.) In 1861, Ballard was fifty-eight years old, a man of political influence and had served as sheriff (1855–56). Hopkins, Smoot or Ballard may not have fired the shot, but they were ardent Southerners involved in the events and fit the local form of wealthy slaveholder.

Enyart's troops had had a hard fight and taken casualties in their first action in the war. And now, by ill chance as they were occupying the town, their color-bearer had been shot down. The shooting of Birch enraged the Federal troops for vengeance as the tide of hatred and counter-enmity and bloodlust that had until then been restrained against the civilians by forces of either side—if only barely—erupted.[111] The Union guide Scragg reported: "The Colonel [Enyart] turned to me and said, 'Mr. Scragg do you have any records in the Court House, I am thinking about burning it.' I replied, 'Yes, my deeds are recorded there, but go ahead and burn it, I don't care.' It was done."[112]

Infuriated, the Federal troops proceeded to retaliate by torching the houses belonging to Confederate sympathizers.[113] Families were forcibly expelled or prevented from returning to their homes, which were set aflame, and women, children and the elderly were left without the means to support themselves. "After sacking all the private houses, they set fire to the village and burned every house, public and private."[114] As the courthouse and town burned, the people of Boone Court House were stricken with horror. Residents watched helplessly as the Federal soldiers allowed the Union militia to remove their vital records from the courthouse before it was burned.[115]

In the course of the war, "Boone was the first victim of this kind of warfare."[116] Within an hour, the entire town, including the courthouse, jail and other buildings, was reduced to ashes—"burned to the ground by the Home Guards," according to some reports. Others attributed the action generically

Union lieutenant colonel David A. Enyart, deputy commander, First Kentucky Infantry Regiment, led the Federal force that burned the town of Boone Court House on September 1, 1861. Before the end of the war, Enyart would rise to the rank of brigadier general fighting under Sherman in the West. *Library of Congress.*

to "the Union force."[117] The insured commercial loss alone was estimated at $40,000, equivalent to over $1 million in 2014 value.[118] The Federal troops gathered all the Southern men in the area in front of the courthouse and tried to persuade them to join the Union cause.[119] Many were rounded up and, when they refused to join, marched off to prison in Charleston.

Neither side, blue nor gray, lingered long in the area after the battle. The Confederates had done their utmost for two days, but the odds were against them from the start. Personal courage and valor could not overcome their material shortcomings, and they hastily retreated to Logan Court House. "The outfit remained there several days until word came that the raiding Federal force had passed out of the county."[120] Enyart proved then and later in the war a fighter, but he was by no means reckless. As there appeared little possibility of bringing the Rebels to battle again, and satisfied that he had accomplished his mission to disperse the Rebel gathering, Enyart decided against pursuit and started the reverse trek to Brownstown on September 2.[121]

Behind them the little armies left a scene of desolate waste, suffering and destruction amid the debris of a battle. Boone Court House lay hideously smoldering in ashes. Where before there had been the town, now there were only the dying flames, charred timbers and blackened ruins of burnt-out buildings and the foul smell of smoke that hung over the countryside. General Wise, enraged by the reports that reached him about the ghastly Federal action, fumed to General Lee that all that remained of Boone Court House was "an old stable" and vowed revenge.[122]

In this sharp, contested battle, "Enyart's march and attack had been rapid and vigorous," and the Confederates were surprised at the boldness of their adversary. In his memoirs, General Cox praised "the terror of the blow."[123] The technical superiority of the Federal weapons, in particular, took a toll. The Rebel militia, "armed with their own weapons of various makes and kinds"—smoothbore flintlock muskets, double-barrel shotguns and hunting rifles ("squirrel guns")—were no match militarily for the stronger and longer-range rifle muskets, artillery and fixed steel bayonets of the Federal soldiers.[124]

To be sure, the hard fact was that rarely during the war were militia auxiliaries on either side able to endure well-led, organized, equipped and disciplined infantry backed by artillery and bayonet charges. The Confederate troops at Boone Court House proved no exception, and the Southern loss was notable, although the casualties in the battle are not known exactly. Sources vary widely; contemporary published estimates at the time

Confederate brigadier general Henry A. Wise, commander, Wise's Legion, vowed revenge against the Union "miscreants" who burned Boone Court House. *Taken from* Battles and Leaders of the Civil War *(1888).*

ranged to more than 125 killed, wounded and captured.[125] Captain Thomas Cox Jr., Company I, First Kentucky Infantry Regiment,[126] commanding the post and reserve at Brownstown, reported the following to Colonel Guthrie on Monday, September 2:

> *I have just had a message from Col. ENYART. The companies of Captains WHEELER and ROOK, with the Home Guards of that vicinity, have had an engagement with the enemy at Boone, totally routing them, after killing 25, taking some prisoners and burning the town. Six of our men were wounded, and I am about to send the ambulance with Dr. WHITE. Our forces will return to-day.*[127]

General Cox, in his official report to Rosecrans, stated that the Rebels were "completely routed" and repeated Captain Cox's report that "twenty-five of the enemy's dead were counted, and it is supposed there are more."[128] First Lieutenant William H. Ross, Company G, Twenty-sixth Ohio Infantry Regiment, reported that the Federals in "a severe engagement, routed the enemy, 450 strong, killed 85 of their number, [and] took five prisoners."[129] Captain Leander H. Long, the chaplain of the Twenty-sixth Ohio Infantry, reported that 60 Confederates were killed in the fight and many others wounded.[130]

The war correspondents kept the telegraph operators busy after the battle, wiring the news of the Union victory to newspapers throughout the North. The *Cincinnati Gazette* and the *New York Times* carried Captain Cox's report to Guthrie and General Cox's report to Rosecrans and the War Department of twenty-five Confederates killed. The *Steubenville Herald* and *Gallipolis Journal* reported, "Thirty-five of their number were known to be killed, and five taken prisoner." The contemporary *Rebellion Record: A Diary of American Events* (1862) would report a Confederate "loss of thirty killed and a large number wounded, and forty prisoners taken."[131]

The *American and Commercial Advertiser* (Baltimore) reported:

> *A fight occurred yesterday at Boone Court House, in the Kanawha region, between a body of Rebels and Federalists, resulting in the total rout of the Rebels with a loss of thirty killed and a large number wounded. Forty were taken prisoners. The Unionists had six wounded but none killed. During the fight the Union men set fire to the town and burned it.*[132]

Newspapers throughout the nation and Europe carried the version of the War Department dispatch that was similarly reported by the *New York Herald* and *New York Sun*, essentially repeating the report of the *New York Times*:

> *There was a fight yesterday at Boone Court House, Virginia, resulting in the total rout of the rebels. Loss thirty killed and a large number wounded; forty prisoners were also taken. None were killed on our side, and but six wounded. Our men burned the town.*[133]

Victor, in his *History of the Southern Rebellion* (1861), recorded: "Rout of rebels at Boone C.H, Western Virginia. A gallant charge made by Captain Wheeler's command; 11 rebels killed and 40 secured as prisoners. The entire village burned."[134] Rees similarly recorded in the *Condensed Chronological*

History of the Great Rebellion (1867): "Enemy routed at Boone C.H., Va., by a brilliant charge of Captain Wheeler's command; 11 rebels killed, and 40 prisoners."[135] Cooper's chronology of the war decades later, which he based on the compilation of statistics from the *Official Records*, military prisons and national cemeteries, reported a total of ten Rebels killed, twenty wounded and thirty captured.[136] The historian Reverend Charles W. Denison of early antislavery fame wrote that the Rebels were "signally defeated," adding that "our troops, fresh and comparatively undisciplined as they were, fought well on this occasion. We drove the enemy at all points, routing them totally, killing thirty, wounding a large number, and taking over forty prisoners."[137]

In the South, the *Tazewell (VA) Democrat* reported the following account:

> *A party of 250 Federals from Kanawha Valley, assisted by about 150 Union men of Boon and vicinity, made a descent upon the Courthouse on Sunday the 1st of September. After sacking all the private houses, they set fire to the village and burned every house, public and private, to the ground, despite the spirited and determined resistance of the Boon and Logan militia. Fortunately most of the records of the county had previously been removed to a place of safety. A Union Company had been formed in the neighborhood of Peytona, which, with other Union men, had threatened to destroy the town, and rob and drive off the Secessionists. To defeat these vile threats, Col. Miller called out the Militia and had the Union Captain, Edward Harless, arrested and confined in jail. This was thought to be the immediate cause of the attack, as the company on hearing of his confinement dispatched a messenger by the name of "Gram" to the Federalists for assistance. Friday night, guided by Union men through the mountain passes, some 250 Federal troops arrived at Peytona, 14 miles from Boone Courthouse. On Saturday the whole force marched to within one mile of the Courthouse and posted themselves on the surrounding mountains, and on Sabbath, about 12 o'clock, destroyed the place. However, they failed to release the Captain, who, together with another Union man, was secured and brought to this place [Tazewell] as a prisoner, and from here taken to Wytheville. The loss of the enemy was 25 killed and as many wounded. Our loss [was] one man killed and four or five slightly wounded. The escape of the militia was miraculous. We gather the above interesting items from a gentleman residing in Boon county.*[138]

In his report of the action to Virginia governor John Letcher, Rebel commander Colonel Miller wrote:

I remained at Camp Boone until the first day of September, 1861, when I was attacked by the enemy, and after an engagement of thirty or thirty-five minutes, finding the enemy too strong my forces were ordered to retreat. In this engagement a part of my command acted bravely, fought the enemy until they were nearly surrounded. In this engagement I had only two men wounded, none killed. The loss to the enemy uncertain, but supposed to be about 60 killed and wounded.[139]

In his renowned history, Stutler reports: "Three of the militiamen were captured, Privates Jesse W. Miller, John Hopkins and Robert Whit."[140] Local tradition, however, supports a large number of Rebels captured and wounded. These included a half dozen Confederate sick and wounded who were perhaps overlooked by the Federals and thus avoided capture. They were discovered by area residents after the battle. Too badly disabled or sick to accompany the Rebels in their haste, they had been left behind at a church at Low Gap, in the bend of the Spruce Fork River below Boone Court House where the Confederate camp had been. The church served as a makeshift hospital after the battle, and there the Confederate surgeon Vandelinde, who had served as a medical corpsman in the trenches at Antwerp (1832) in the Belgian Revolution, performed the grim business of amputating destroyed limbs that could not be saved.[141]

If he was there, the Rebel "Devil Anse" Hatfield escaped. In addition, how and when Virginia state senator William Pate escaped after the defeat at Boone Court House is not known, but he got away. Pate made his way "into Wyoming county, and there endeavored to raise forces to go to the relief of the citizens of Boone, but found it of no avail. On the contrary; he was informed that efforts were being made to organize Union companies."[142]

Various reports cited that among the captured at Boone Court House were a large number of "contrabands"—the military term for captured or escaped slaves and those who affiliated with Union military forces. How many slaves were captured and taken away to the Kanawha Valley was not reported, but in 1860, only 36 out of about 750 families in Boone County owned slaves, who made up 3 percent of the population. The 1860 U.S. census placed the population of the county at 4,840 overall, including about 158 slaves.[143] Although Boone County was not home to a large concentration of slaves, most were concentrated along the Big and Little Coal Rivers, where rich bottomlands encouraged farming. Those owned together by the Ballard, Hopkins and Smoot clans alone in the vicinity of Boone Court House numbered many dozens of slaves.

After the Union army occupied the Kanawha Valley in the summer of 1861, there were many dramatic instances of slaves who used the arrival of Federal troops to escape bondage. A large camp arose at Malden, where several thousand slaves labored in the saltworks throughout the war.[144] One account with a tragic ending was associated with the Battle of Boone Court House:

> *Henry H. Hopkins is a notorious Secessionist living near Coal River, and a man of considerable property. Some time before his arrest he sent the negro man mentioned in the complaint South, in charge of some Logan County "bushwhackers." On his way and in McDowell County the man managed to escape and returned into Hopkins's neighborhood, near Boone C.H, where he took his wife and three children alleged to have been the property of a woman named Smoot, and brought them to this post. Upon his representation that he had escaped from armed rebels in McDowell County, and without further knowledge of the facts, the Post Quartermaster set him at work. About the 19th of February Hopkins came to town with Mrs. Smoot, and without notice to the quartermaster or any color of authority by any civil process, procured the aid of Kelly, the jailer, seized the negro and took him to Wright's hotel. The provost-marshal, knowing that Hopkins was an active Secessionist and that he had been personally engaged in the combat at Boone C.H. last fall, ordered his arrest. Shortly after, he was waited upon by B.F. Smith, Esq., U.S. District Attorney, who stated that he had known Mr. Hopkins for a good many years and was confident he was a good Union man, although in fact the deputy-marshal at the very time held a warrant for the arrest of Hopkins for treason and conspiracy, under an indictment found in the U.S. Court, of which, to say the least of it, it is very strange Mr. Smith should have been ignorant. At the request of the provost-marshal, the warrant was served on Hopkins, who was admitted to bail in the sum of $2,000, which is most inadequate security for the appearance of a man of Hopkins's wealth and influence, accused of such a crime. After the arrest of Hopkins, the negro being left to himself returned to his quarters, but sometime during the night stole a skiff and attempted to escape with his family down the Kanawha River. The circumstances of his accident in the river, the drowning of his family and his subsequent capture, I have not been able to investigate fully.*[145]

Beyond the Confederate soldiers and slaves captured, the *Official Records* and other sources indicate that a number of pro-secessionist citizens were also taken prisoner, which largely depopulated the town of men and caused great suffering for their families. Those who expressed or were identified by the Union militia as showing sympathy to the Confederacy were arrested. Whatever the number captured, the prisoners were taken to Charleston, where at least some were tried for insurrection.[146] Some were released and allowed to return home, while others were jailed and indicted for treason. Some were exchanged. The captured citizens included members of the large, prominent pro-secessionist and slaveholding families.[147] Yet others were sent to the Federal prison at Camp Chase, Ohio, where at least one of the Rebel soldiers captured in the fight at Boone Court House died.[148]

Some prisoners might not even have reached Charleston. The war in western Virginia was marked for its savagery, as both sides early on adopted a "no prisoners" policy.[149] As events proved in the Coal River Valley, neither side needed encouragement in this particular way of war. The Twenty-sixth Ohio Regiment's Private Deasy later wrote about events concerning the Federal descent on Boone Court House and his company's return to the Kanawha Valley: "The detachment was in charge of Capt Wheeler…Col. Guthrie (I think that was the name of the Colonel of the 1st Ky.) told Capt. Wheeler that he wanted no prisoners; that it was a bad man who was not worth a pound of lead, and so we took no prisoners except one on our way back to Charleston, W.Va."[150]

The Federals seized twenty-two horses; a large quantity of arms, including muskets, double-barreled shotguns and hunting rifles; wagons; and camp equipment. The two Federal militia officers who had been confined in the jail were not recovered. The Rebels had already sent them to Tazewell and thence to Richmond.[151] The Twenty-sixth Ohio Infantry companies reported that the Federal losses were none killed and six wounded, including, as it turned out, the flag-waving color-bearer, whose wound soon proved mortal. Corporal Nowlin received a severe wound in the breast while leading the Union militia. (In recognition of his role at Boone Court House, Nowlin was officially appointed first lieutenant of the newly created Company B, Eighth West Virginia Infantry Regiment.)[152]

The traditional estimate for casualties at Boone Court House, cited for the past century, of six Union troops wounded and two Confederates wounded and six captured has become iconic. The estimate, though widely cited, is faulty. Throughout the war, neither the Union nor the Confederacy kept standardized aggregate records of casualties. The traditional estimate of the battle's casualties was based on the absence of or, at best, incomplete, fragmentary and often contradictory reports. This was especially so for the Confederate army and for militia and irregular units in particular. Despite best efforts, however, since historical casualty data in the Civil War is seldom reliable, in many cases often all that are available are overall casualties rather than a breakdown of killed, wounded and captured. This is frequently the case with the numerous period sources concerning Confederate casualties at Boone Court House, for which the historical record includes at least fifteen variations of total Confederate casualties, ranging from 1 to 125 killed, wounded and captured.

The most interesting difference between the traditional consensus figure and a higher estimate of casualties for Boone Court House includes the result of underreported deaths, particularly Confederate. In fact, there were at least four recorded deaths, including men killed in action and those who died later. At least four Federal and Confederate soldiers either died on the battlefield at Boone Court House or later from their wounds in a hospital or in a prisoner of war camp. These included Confederate private James E. Pauley, killed at Red House; Private Birch, the Company G, Twenty-sixth Ohio Infantry flag-bearer who was wounded at Boone Court House and died of his wounds in the hospital on September 26 at Gallipolis, Ohio; and Confederate private Jesse W. Miller, who was captured at Boone Court House and died of disease in the Federal prisoner of war pen at Camp Chase, Ohio, on October 12.[153] And during the return to Charleston, a Twenty-sixth Ohio Infantry soldier's gun accidentally discharged, killing him.[154] In addition, the First Kentucky Infantry suffered at least one wounded.[155]

To be sure, the Federal soldiers of the Ohio and Kentucky units were not the only casualties. All things considered, although no confirmed record has been located detailing overall Home Guard casualties, some are known to have occurred in the fighting at Boone Court House.[156] Local tradition, not supported by other evidence, has it that the Union militia suffered two to three dozen casualties, killed and wounded. These included Union volunteer Private Robert Mitchell, who was wounded.[157] There were undoubtedly other Union militia casualties. Official Confederate reports estimated that Union casualties totaled fifty to sixty-one combined Union army and militia killed and wounded. These included Colonel Miller's estimate that the Federals suffered sixty casualties and Captain William Baisden's report that the Federals lost sixty-one killed and wounded.[158] The *Tazewell (VA) Democrat* reported "25 killed and as many wounded."[159]

Earlier accounts (including Colonel Miller's report to Richmond) also excluded the action, and therefore the casualties, of the Confederate attack at Red House on August 31. The difference between the traditional estimate of Confederate casualties at Boone Court House and the higher overall figure includes clarifying among the diversity of historical accounts the mixture of killed or captured on or near the field of battle as a result of hostile action, wounds or illness. A reasonable modern estimate of the casualties among the military personnel at Boone Court House, therefore, is currently established for the Union as at least eleven total, including two dead and nine wounded. The most recent estimate of the Confederate military casualties is twenty-five total, including killed, wounded and captured.[160] As analysis of Civil War casualties continues to improve with computerization, and the individual fates of all troops in the war becomes better known, the number of known casualties at Boone Court House will likely grow.

For now, however, casualty estimations remain imprecise. Civil War statistician Thomas L. Livermore calculated that generally in Civil War fighting, excluding captured, there was about 1.0 soldier killed for every 2.5 wounded in battle.[161] Throughout the historical records, both official and unofficial, one of the more consistent numbers cited for Confederate casualties in the Battle of Boone Court House is twenty-five total military casualties. That is presently the consensus estimate. Subtracting from this estimate of twenty-five total Confederate military casualties five captured—another of the most consistent numbers cited for the Battle of Boone Court House—leaves twenty killed and wounded. Applying Livermore's rule (rounded up) yields an estimate for the Confederate military loss at Boone Court House of five dead, fifteen wounded and five captured. This breakdown is remarkably close to some historical estimates of six dead and fourteen wounded.[162]

In addition, the historical records frequently also cite many private citizens at Boone Court House captured as political prisoners and slaves taken as contraband. These references help explain the variously large and widely separated estimates for the number of Confederates who were captured, which range in disparate reports from one to forty (another commonly cited number). The variable estimates are attributable to the sources including and excluding different mixtures of types of casualties in their estimates. Certainly, including political prisoners and slaves, of which there were many taken in the overall Confederate numbers, helps account for the larger number of variously reported Confederate captured than can be accounted for purely among military units at this time.

These include numerous references to political prisoners and slaves captured in the *Official Records*, newspapers, government sources and participant reports. For example, a few months after the battle, a delegate to the First Constitutional Convention of West Virginia in Wheeling noted:

At the battle of Boone Courthouse a prisoner was taken, a respectable, good, honest and humble citizen—for I had occasion to know him—with a worthy family, depending entirely upon his labors and exertions. He was taken in battle with his gun in his hand and with a load in the gun; and when he was carried to Kanawha a prisoner by the Federal troops, I was sent for to see him; and as the tears streamed down his cheeks he detailed to me the circumstances in which he was brought into this calamity; with his family helpless and almost houseless, and without the means of sustenance in his absence, he doomed to a long incarceration at Camp Chase, Ohio, until the fortunes of war may return him to his family. He said he was a Union man and had been a Union man. He lived in a secession neighborhood; the colonel of the county had called upon the militia under the law of the State to come forth to rally against these invaders; and these leaders called him, and they further told him if he did not rally to that call and did not obey the law he might expect as the penalty to be shot.[163]

For these reasons, although presently impossible to catalogue the fate of each of the one thousand or more men who fought at Boone Court House in September 1861, analysis in the last decade or so indicates that the battle's total Confederate casualties numbered about fifty-seven, including at least two killed, nine wounded and eleven captured in addition to thirty-five political prisoners and slaves. This count, four times higher than the commonly cited historical figure of fourteen, is immanently derived when the many historical references to political prisoners and captured slaves are included. These also help explain a local tradition that, over one hundred years later, bitterly characterized the Federal action as a "raid" in which the victors rounded up and took captive a large number of residents sympathetic to the Confederacy and mercilessly plundered property and livestock in the area.

Indeed, the Federals sacked the town itself and swept the countryside, appropriating horses, mules and cattle.[164] During the return trip to the Kanawha Valley, the column of Federal soldiers and their prisoners, captured livestock and wagon train filled with the contents of plunder gathered during the expedition spread out on the Boone–Logan road. Many years later, an old man who witnessed the spectacle when he was a boy told his granddaughter about it. A veritable "trail of tears," when the head of the snake-like column reached the foot of Drawdy Mountain, its tail stretched three miles to Newport, lengthened by stragglers with loot and a parade of demoralized and terrified women and children following family members who had been taken prisoner.[165]

The starvation and deprivation that followed in the area in the forthcoming difficult first autumn and winter of the war were largely attributable to the grim Federal action.[166] The "trail of tears" makes a dramatic statement about why the Battle of Boone Court House became so central a moment in Coal River Valley history. The battle and its aftermath, taken together, help explain the devastating and humiliating experience and why it was forever burned in local memory.

On their return to the Kanawha Valley, the Federal troops were met at Peytona "by a party of ladies, who had formed themselves into a company of Union Home Guards. The boys lent them their muskets, and they were put through the facings by one of the officers, who speaks very highly of their proficiency in drill. The boys, after giving nine hearty cheers for the patriotic ladies of Peytona, took up their line of march for Charleston."[167]

Union private William Van Buren Bias, Spurlock's Company (A), Peytona Home Guards; later sergeant, Company B, Eighth (West) Virginia Infantry Regiment; and first lieutenant, Seventh West Virginia Cavalry. *Library of Congress.*

A large number of the militia enlisted for Federal service at Peytona on September 2.[168] Among the volunteers was Methodist minister Private William Van Buren Bias, of Drawdy Creek and Spurlock's company of the Peytona Home Guards. In 1865, Bias would become the county's first elected sheriff.[169] "These troops remained in the Peytona area for about 10 days protecting the Union recruiters and citizens from retaliation by outraged Confederate sympathizers."[170] At Brownstown, they boarded the steamboats that returned them downstream to the Union army camp at Charleston.[171]

In the following days, as the threat of Confederate reprisals directed at Peytona grew and persisted, General Cox reinforced the Union force by dispatching Company K of the Twenty-sixth Ohio Regiment to depart "from Charleston and return to Peytona accompanied by the 1st Kentucky." Company K remained at Peytona until September 8, when it returned to the Kanawha Valley. "Meanwhile, on September 5, Company G was ordered to march from Charleston to the Little Coal River. After two days on a circuitous route via Mud Creek and then to Peytona, Company G" also returned to the Kanawha Valley on September 11.[172] Guthrie also dispatched a battalion of the First Kentucky regiment to raid the Big Coal River Valley.

At the time, the Boone Court House action was noted among the important and strategic moments thus far in the war.[173] Wartime historian Denison wrote that the results of "the contest there speedily convinced the rebels that the Union would not consent to allow any part of the Old Dominion it could control to pass, without a struggle, under the black flag of secession."[174] Moved by the accounts of the bloodshed, an anonymous Union poet penned a patriotic and sentimental work published during the war in a book of patriotic verse in the North:

DEAD IN HIS YOUTH.
AT THE FIGHT AT BOONE COURT HOUSE, VA.,
September 1st, '61.

THE earliest ray of morn had brought
The din of arms to many an ear,
And many a life was quickly bought
And fitted for the narrow bier.
For hours the flash of muskets gleamed
Along our ranks, from line to line—
For hours our shining bayonets beamed
Like shifting spray upon the brine.

The day that flushed the summer sky
At length had faded into night,
And many a star had risen high
And dropp'd on earth its rays of light;
The pale moon rose above the hills,
And coldly smiled upon the plain—
Its rays were riding on each rill,
And resting on each battle-slain.

But one whose brow was young with years,
Lies where the moonbeams kiss his brow!
Oh! ye who never shed warm tears,
Come gaze—and shed them now.
See where the bullet pierced him through,
And laid him in the pool of gore!
Upon his brow the pearly dew
Of life will settle there no more.

This lad, he as his vine-clad hills
To seek the treacherous battle-plain,
Where flows the blood like mountain rills
From many a stalwart hero slain!
He was the first within the fray,
The dash, the charge, or fight,
But now his brow of marble clay
In death is ashy, cold and white.

Alas! that cruel death should take
The life that filled his noble breast.
And sad that such a heart should break
To take its last and only rest.
When parents watch for his return,
His vine-clad hills among,
O! how their hearts will beat and burn
To learn that he will ne'er come home.

Alas! I wonder if that heart will break
Within his aged mother's breast,
When she shall learn her son's sad fate,

And where he takes his lonely rest?
Alas! for her, the gentle maid,
Who lonely waits his fond return!
She soon shall know that 'neath the shade,
The pine tree is her lover's urn.

—*Anonymous*[175]

The lively engagement marked the farthest southward advance of the Union army thus far in the war. The Confederates were driven from the town and withdrew from the Coal River Valley, and the honors of the day rested with the Federal troops. Yet they stopped short of reaping the full success that was in their grasp as the result of the hard fighting they had done. The Southern troops, raised and commanded by Colonel Miller, stood up to the Federal "invasion" by attacking first at Red House on the outskirts of Boone Court House. Then, the next day, for a half hour, the Rebels held at bay in forlorn hope a largely superior force they believed outnumbered them six to one. Nonetheless, the presumed invincibility of their fastness in the mountainous region had been badly shaken.

It is impossible to overestimate the profound influence of the Battle of Boone Court House on the war's prosecution in southern West Virginia. With the firm base of operations he had established at Brownstown along the Kanawha, Enyart's delivery to General Cox of the victory at Boone Court House opened the road to Logan. On both sides, the small fight was remarkable for its examples of daring and courage—the Confederates, though from the outset at a heavy disadvantage, attacking first at the plains of Little Coal, and the Federals the next day seizing the round top, charging and fording the river under fire. The Union victory caused a tremendous outpouring of patriotic fervor in the North and proportionately outraged the South. Finally, and foremost, the affair was remarkable for the ghastly burning of Boone Court House and the misery inflicted on the local population. As a consequence, Southern sympathizers throughout the region seethed for vengeance.[176]

Chapter 3

COAL RIVER

The appearance of the first formation of Federal troops in the Coal River Valley threw the population into consternation. The Battle of Boone Court House had been won by the Union army and its local militia allies—the Peytona and Pond Fork Home Guard companies, for the most part. The outcome was that the county seat had been burned to the ground and the Federals or their Unionist militia allies were generally in contested control of the region. They had constructed defenses at various places, including a post at Peytona and a mountainside fort of log, rock and earthen works at Pond Fork to protect themselves against Confederate movement and attack and marauders, as well as to impose control of these important passes through the mountains in order to enable Federal movement in the region.

Early in September, after the fight at Boone Court House, another force of Union troops was sent into the Big Coal River country. In this case, since there was no large body of Confederate troops organizing or operating in the Big Coal country, it seems that the object was primarily to brutalize the citizenry who were loyal to the South in order to deter their enthusiasm for supporting the rebellion. In fact, General Cox's strategy was terror, as he openly said about the Boone Court House expedition.[177] Now it was the Big Coal's turn.

Captain David Y. Johns, Company D, First Kentucky Infantry Regiment, departed from Brownstown at the head of a train of wagons defended by a battalion of five companies of infantry and a section of artillery, about five hundred men. The Federals marched southward to the Big Coal River along

A view of the Big Coal River as seen along the West Virginia Route 3 state highway. *Library of Congress.*

present-day West Virginia State Route 3 to ravage in Boone and Raleigh Counties, and as a consequence, many homesteads were sacked.

The organization of the Union force was as follows:

First Kentucky Infantry Regiment, Cox's Kanawha Brigade, West Virginia, Department of the Ohio

Company B, Captain Alva R. Hadlock
Company D, Captain David Y. Johns
Company F, Captain Jesse J. Stepleton
Company I, Captain Thomas Cox Jr.
Company K, Captain John F. Becker

First Kentucky Light Artillery

Simmonds' Battery, Captain Seth J. Simmonds[178]

Meanwhile, the main forces of the Union and Confederate armies in the Kanawha Valley remained engaged in the ongoing strategically important struggle for Gauley Bridge. There, Union general Cox and Confederate general Wise's forces battled for Cotton Hill, the high ground that thoroughly dominated the militarily significant town. While thus occupied, the Rebel camp at Cotton Hill received the news of the Union raiding force—"old Abe's hen-roost robbers"—marching into Boone County, this time headed toward Raleigh County and accompanied and aided again by their "Federal hirelings," the Peytona Home Guards who joined the force at Mouth of Short Creek.[179]

This bold move directly threatened Raleigh Court House, and when he learned the Federal raiders were tearing up the Big Coal region, General Wise immediately selected a force of cavalry and hastened the Confederates to intercept the raiders. He directed them to counter-raid Brownstown if possible and "scout the Kanawha valley, harass the enemy, and chastise those traitors (Union men) who had been annoying the true and loyal men on and near the river."[180] Wise detached six companies of Southern cavalry under Colonel James Lucius Davis, Wise's Legion's First Virginia Cavalry Regiment, and in command of all the cavalry operating in the area of southern (West) Virginia that General Wise commanded. It was a fast-moving, formidable cavalry force from which Wise expected significant results.

Lucius Davis slipped out of Hamilton (Fayette County) toward Raleigh Court House. The companies that left with Davis on September 10 were Pate, Phelps, Jordan, Rosser, McGruder and Poague's cavalry. At Fayette

Court House, they were joined by Caskie's Rangers, and at the head of these combined 240 Rebel cavalry, Davis struck southward.[181] In his command were men who would go on to play bigger roles in the war, especially company commanders Henry Clay Pate, Robert A. Caskie and Lieutenant Julius G. Tucker. Both Pate and Caskie went on to command their own cavalry regiments during the war, while Tucker later commanded a Confederate regiment of Federal turncoats.

The organization of the Confederate force that Wise sent to the Coal River Valley was as follows:

First Cavalry Regiment, Wise's Legion, Colonel James Lucius Davis and Lieutenant Colonel John N. Clarkson

Company A (Caskie's Mounted Rangers), Captain Robert A. Caskie
Company C (Rockbridge Rangers) Captain George W. Jordan
Company D (Pate's Rangers, also known as the Letcher Mounted Guards and Petersburg Rangers), Captain Henry C. Pate
Company G (Jackson Rangers), Captain Edgar C. Phelps
Company H (Valley Rangers, also known as the Rockingham Cavalry), Captain George Poague
Company I (Henrico Light Dragoons), Captain Zachariah S. McGruder
Company K (Rosser's Mounted Rangers, also known as the Virginia Rangers and Virginia Texas Rangers), Captain J. Travis Rosser[182]

Colonel Davis, forty-eight, had graduated from West Point in 1833. From Henrico, Virginia, he served in the U.S. Army as a lieutenant in the Fourth U.S. Artillery from 1833 to 1836. By 1850, he was a leading citizen in Henrico County and was lieutenant colonel of the Fourth Virginia Cavalry Militia (1858–60). In April 1861, he captained the Henrico Troop, a company of volunteer cavalry. He had published a book called *The Trooper's Manual: or, Tactics for Light Dragoons and Mounted Riflemen* (Richmond, VA: A. Morris, 1861), which the Confederate army had adopted as its cavalry manual.

A cousin of Confederate president Jefferson Davis, the First Virginia Cavalry commander was known for tireless energy and his tendency to work troops hard:

Accordingly that cavalry moved from its rendezvous, at Fayette courthouse, on the 11th, and marched by bridle paths over the steep mountains of that wild region, struck the head waters of Loop creek, crossed to Cole river, and

Confederate cavalry on the move. *Taken from* Battles and Leaders of the Civil War *(1888)*.

passed the numerous rocky fords of that rapid stream, and were closing their laborious march, when the night set in with rain and darkness.[183]

Arriving at Raleigh Court House, Davis learned that the Federal companies were at work raiding along the Boone-Raleigh frontier: "The enemy had been acting as brigands in the valley, stealing every species of property, insulting women, taking men and little boys prisoners. Among the property taken ought to be mentioned cattle, horses, Negroes, etc."[184]

By hard riding, Davis spurred his cavalry force forward to close with the enemy before they were across Lens Creek Mountain and would be safe from pursuit. "Despite the inclemency of the weather, the jaded troopers were soon in their saddles and on the track of the enemy, although the strength of the foe was, according to report, double their number."[185] If the Confederate force could catch the Federals and engage before they got back across Lens Creek Mountain, perhaps the entire Federal force could be destroyed. "It was with difficulty that the eager troopers could find their way in darkness and storm, through the rocks and fords of a swollen river."[186] In order for the Confederates to reach the Federals,

the Coal River was forded ninety-seven times during the night of the 11ᵗʰ inst., under a violent storm of rain, and in the darkness so profound that one's hand was invisible. A torch had to be used at every crossing of the river. The Laurel Mountain had to be crossed in file, without a horse falling or a man dismounting, where no one before, even among the inhabitants of that mountain, had ever dared to thread this rugged, steep, and precipitous path on horseback.

For many miles the road was overhung by the loftiest precipices and skirted by impenetrable thickets of the laurel, and in the very region where the traitorous sons of Virginia and marauding Yankees had collected for ambush, plunder, and blood. Though in the nest of traitors, our men, with the rapids of the river boiling at their feet, a violent storm howling over their head, the utter darkness rendered still deeper by the glare of the torch, with fearless hearts and good wills, continued the journey through the most broken and wild scenery of Western Virginia.[187]

About 3:00 a.m. on September 12 at Jarrolds Valley (present-day Whitesville), Colonel Davis learned that the Federals had pillaged and sacked Pack's plantation, were stealing cattle and were camped there about two miles away at present-day Sylvester, then called Pack's Branch or Lower Round Bottom. Augustus Pack was one of the Coal River Valley's most affluent landowners with various tracts in Boone, Raleigh and other counties totaling over fifteen thousand acres. With fifteen slaves, he was the county's second-largest individual slaveholder. Along with the Toneys and Hopkinses, the Packs were one of the most Confederate families in Boone County. They gave food and supplies to the Confederate army, had several family members in the Confederate service and therefore were targets of Union attention.

Confederate colonel James Lucius Davis, First Cavalry Regiment commander, Wise's Legion, Virginia Cavalry, led the Confederate force that was victorious in the Battle of Coal River on September 12, 1861. *OpenLibrary.org.*

But until he knew the strength that the Federals could muster at Pack's plantation, Colonel Davis could not determine whether to attack. He sent scouts forward to learn what they could from local residents. The scouts returned with word that "the enemy would be found numbering about five hundred" at Pack's and that the wagon train was moving down the valley beyond a few miles distant. Davis "determined to attack even that force" although the Confederate cavalrymen would be outnumbered by more than two to one.[188] Davis reasoned, "We had traveled a long way, and, not being expected, would easily surprise them. So, never minding the rain a moment, we continued our march through the night, and at daybreak surrounded Pack's place…"[189]

Upon arrival at Pack's, however, about daylight, the Confederate cavalrymen discovered that the Union train and guard had withdrawn the previous afternoon after plundering Lower Round Bottom, "together with 200 head of cattle" and a number of horses "which they had stolen from different parties, and were driving towards the Federal camp" at Brownstown.[190] In the face of this development, Colonel Davis did an amazing thing. It was late in the day, and the cavalry had traversed, in twenty-four hours, a distance of about seventy-five miles over steep mountain trails, bridle paths and rocky slopes in wretched weather. The Confederate cavalry commander "immediately ordered his command in pursuit" and divided his small force in two. "Not halting, the word of march was given, and the column moved on briskly at a trot cut, Pate's company in advance."[191] Davis held back Caskie and McGruder's companies in reserve with him. He sent Clarkson racing ahead with four companies (those of Phelps, Jordan, Rosser and Poague) to chase down and overtake the Federals on the Coal River Road and attack their rear.[192]

In Captain Henry Clay Pate, Davis placed a firebrand in the van. Nationally prominent in the prewar period as a pro-slavery legalist and propagandist, Pate knew the land intimately since his widowed mother and two brothers lived at Mouth of Short Creek. The cavalry under Pate were among the better-mounted and armed Confederate horsemen in western Virginia with swords and Jenks-Remington model 1845 U.S. Navy breech-loading carbines. These were weapons "Pate fished up from the water, into which they had been thrown from the old ship *Pennsylvania*, at Norfolk. They are in excellent condition, and very convenient to handle, being breech-loading and self-priming weapons. They will also shoot a long distance."[193]

After twelve miles at full gallop, Colonel Clarkson's detachment came upon Federal stragglers near Coon's Mill (present-day Seth on West Virginia Route 3). They "learned that the enemy camped there, and was not far ahead," seemingly unmindful of the Rebel presence.[194] Clarkson seized the situation at a glance. It was growing late in the day, and both the Rebel

Confederate cavalry charge. Excellent riders and shots and reckless in the saddle, the Confederate cavalry in the Coal River mountains in autumn 1861 exhibited horsemanship and fighting spirit. Led by colorful and capable commanders, the Southern cavalry arm achieved noteworthy victories at Coal River and Pond Fork. *Library of Congress.*

troopers and their horses were exhausted by the exertions of the arduous sortie from Hamilton. But the opportunity at hand raised Confederate hopes that they could cut off and capture the entire Union force, and the risk appeared worth the additional effort despite the late hour.

> *At this point we commenced the gallop, and an advance of five of Capt. Pate's men were sent on ahead for scouting. In a few moments they captured a wagon, team and two prisoners. Here the chase became spirited. Our men raised a yell as straggler after straggler was overtaken, which was repeated by the whole column. Seeing that the main body would probably hear our shouts and be apprised of our coming, the gallop was increased to a fiercer charge and for three miles the race was terrific, and at a time bid fair to end in more damage to us than the enemy. The road was wretched, narrow and crooked, and had one leading horse fallen, twenty or fifty would have tumbled together and an indefinite number of limbs and necks had been broken.* [195]

Clarkson ordered Captain Rosser, whose command appeared in the best condition, to detach from the column and race from Coon's Mill with his company to prevent the Federals from escaping and to attack their rear.

Then the wildest excitement moved the troops. Captain Rosser, with his company, were ordered to take the lead in the pursuit and charge, and off in full strain dashed along his splendid command. Every man gave a shout—some the Indian war-whoop—and as the column swept along, like a thunder-cloud driven by the angry winds of heaven, shouting the war-cry of victory, the true women and girls of Virginia, on many a farm along the road, with tearful eyes, clapped their hands with joy, crying out, "A few more miles, Southern soldiers, and the enemy are yours!" These tidings gave fresh impulse to all, and the horses catching the inspiration of their riders, the mountains seemed to swell with the loud shouts of the men, and the sound of the horses' hoofs up and down many a steep hill.[196]

After a few more miles at full gallop, splashing through the Big Coal's creeks, Rosser's cavalry "came in sight of them."[197] "At this time, Pate's and Rosser's men were pretty well mixed up," and Phelps, whose company was aligned in the rear of the column, had gone ahead with Rosser.[198] Together, these were the first Confederate cavalrymen to arrive on the scene as Rosser took command for the South at the beginning of the battle. The comparatively larger body of Federals was involved in quietly establishing camp for the evening on the broad plain at the mouth of Joes Creek on the right bank of the Big Coal River, about two and half miles southeast of Mouth of Short Creek.

The Union infantry were posted in an apple orchard and an open riverside field, ground suitable for cavalry action. From the disposition of the Federals, it appeared that they were unmindful of the Rebels' presence. In all, in addition to seventeen civilian prisoners—mostly Pack's family and slaves—the Federals had in tow the cattle as well as horses, mules and wagons loaded with corn and other plunder raided from homesteads and communities up and down the Big Coal.[199] The long line of wagons stretched toward Brownstown, making snail-like progress along the almost impassable road to Brownstown. A Rebel participant reported, "When we came on the rascals at Mrs. Tony's, they were in the act of drawing out, to carry off, the carriage of Mrs. Pate, which she had sent there for safe keeping."[200]

From their position on the low hill, the Confederate van watched in suspense. If they could make a supreme effort, they might block the Union force's return to the Kanawha, sever it from General Cox's army and capture or disperse it. A few hours of daylight yet remained.

View of the northern part of the Battle of Coal River battlefield at the mouth of Toney's Branch (present-day Bloomingrose) on the Big Coal River, about fifty years after the Civil War. The Coal River Road, in the foreground, was the main route for frequent raids into Boone County and beyond during the war. *West Virginia Geological Survey (1915)*.

Rosser determined not to wait for the balance of the Confederate cavalry and instead attack immediately. Rosser knew he must bring on a battle before the Federals could organize for defense, even though Clarkson, with his companies, had not arrived on the scene. That was the purpose of Clarkson sending Rosser forward by himself with his company—to surprise the Federals and force them into battle. Rosser had accomplished both these missions. The Battle of Coal River had begun, and the combat that followed was probably as desperate as any in that cavalry on either side had taken part thus far in the war. The Confederates "all fought with that intrepidity that none but the true sons of the South could, to drive a ruthless and savage foe from our homes and firesides."[201]

Classically, Rosser's cavalry tactics were not based on weight of numbers or the fire he could bring to bear but rather on speed. His plan was to strike a stunning blow at the beginning of the fight before the Federals could effectively react. Seemingly, his intention was, by shock, to scatter the enemy troops and drive them pell-mell down the valley, into the river and against the mountains. As Captain Cox later expressed it, the Federal infantry had not been "expecting or anticipating any such attack," and the Confederates "came down on them like a thunderbolt from the heavens."[202] Nothing could withstand the charge of the Rebel cavalry. Pate and Rosser's men "pitched into the Yankees right and left, riding amongst them, and without dismounting at first, shooting them as if they were a herd of wild goats."[203] With this background in mind, the chaotic nature of the battle becomes understandable.

During the early part of the battle, the surprised Federal soldiers "showed fight at the beginning." They held their ground and tried to make a stand in the orchard and field. But it was only temporary. Rosser's "boys poured such volleys of lead into them" that the Federal resolve shortly gave way, and Rosser formed his cavalry in line of battle and gave the order "Charge!" His company, "aided by half a dozen dashing bold soldiers from the other companies," surged forward in their stirrups. Down swept the cavalry at a thunderous gallop as they made a violent charge against the Union line.[204] The charge was daring, spectacular and, by accounts, devastating. The Rebel horsemen went in on the gallop, sabers swinging, the cavalry shouting the invincible "Rebel yell." The charge "scattered the Hessians, who retired, leaving the ground covered with the dead and dying."[205] The fight that ensued in this battle was severe with instances of hand-to-hand combat as riflemen swung their weapons as war clubs with death-dealing effects.[206]

From various reports, it would appear that Captain Cox, upon seeing the Confederates on the road above the Union camp, managed to form his company (I) before Rosser broke through and dispersed the Union force defending from capture or destruction the livestock and wagon train loaded with supplies invaluable to the Confederate army. It would further seem that Johns and Cox's two companies—D and I—together managed to stand up and resist the Rebel onslaught long enough at least to enable largely the remainder of the forlorn Union force to escape. This appears so because, of the five companies and the artillery that made up the Federal force, these two companies would account for three-fourths of the troops who were captured, more than the rest of the command's casualties combined. Simmonds' artillery lost only one man captured, which suggests the cannoneers got away in time to avoid capture.[207] (See Table 1)

Table 1
Casualties, First Kentucky Infantry Regiment,
Coal River, September 12, 1861

Unit	Captured	Pct. of Total
Company B	1	2%
Company D	22	47%
Company F	1	2%
Company I	13	28%
Company K	6	13%
Simmonds' Battery	1	2%
Unknown	3	6%
	47	100%

Numbering about sixty troopers, the van of the Confederate cavalry pursuit force came riding down the Coal River Road and, suddenly and unexpectedly, burst upon the Federal soldiers, who outnumbered them outrageously eight to one. Sixty against over five hundred could only be characterized as impudence. As the Confederates fiercely attacked, the most serious fighting of the day resulted in a general mêlée of men, horses, cattle, mules and wagons. "The Southern onset was so violent and sudden, that the marauders were routed in fifteen minutes," the Federal infantry falling back in a confused and broken mass. Thus, the Federals stood up as best they could under the pressure of this charge. They held their ground as the cavalry rode through and over them, sabering the Federals, and then passed on, leaving the Union companies defending the wagon train well in the rear.

At some point in the swirling confusion of the attack, Captain Johns and a small group of men seemingly became cut off from his company and felt now that while he could not save his command, he could save, at least, a portion of his troops on the field by scattering. Taking advantage of a break, he withdrew with a handful of troops and ordered them to escape as rapidly as possible to the mountains. When he and the men with him fled into the Coal River Mountain hills, some dozens remained under command of Captain Cox, left behind to hold off the Confederates until the wagon train would be safe from pursuit if possible. The Union force thus was beaten, left to make its way, every man for himself as best he could. As unit after unit broke and the Confederate cavalry rode them down, their ranks were driven from the field, and Federal soldiers "ran in all directions, leaving all of their plunder behind."[208]

Union private Charles Webber, of Company I, First Kentucky Infantry, reported that "Captain Johns, of Company D, in command, immediately fled, leaving the men to fight. The battle lasted for some time, when the men, having no officer to command them, gave way and retreated to the mountains."[209] A sergeant in Company D, First Kentucky Infantry, refuted "the cowardice of Captain Johns. He says the Captain did not run until he discovered the enemy attempting to out-flank him, and as their number was superior, he deemed it prudent to take to the mountains, which he did, with a squad of his men."[210]

Regardless, after the Union ranks broke, the retreat became a rout, which continued for three miles down the Big Coal River Valley. In the three-hour running action, the remainder of the follow on Confederate companies rushed into the action piecemeal as they arrived on the scene—Jordan's, Pate's, Poague's and, lastly, Phelps' companies. The battle moved from field to field along the Coal River Road toward Mouth of Short Creek. Cavalry charges were made by the Confederates and received by isolated Federals, who tried to make a stand, only to be captured or cut down as they sought safety in flight.

The pursuit of the Federal remnants continued to the mouth of Toney's Branch (present-day Bloomingrose), about one and a quarter miles east of Mouth of Short Creek and within twelve miles of Brownstown. Overtaken at Toney's, the remainder of the Federals were "entirely routed and driven up the wood in the mountains, with a heavy loss of killed and wounded."[211] The cavalry made a final charge on the town of Peytona but were repulsed by Lieutenant Andrew J. Hogan, Company I, with a squad of the Peytona Home Guards belonging to the town.[212] The retreat was not pressed farther. Clarkson's troopers were exhausted and their numbers insufficient to corral the entire Federal force, whose fugitives had scattered.

Lieutenant Colonel Clarkson, who had been delayed on the road, reached the scene of action as "the enemy were flying up the wood for concealment and escape."

> *It is due to Captain Rosser to state that this brilliant skirmish was won while he had command; and on two most important occasions, and in the thickest part of the fight, he was nearest to the enemy. At one time, far ahead of everyone he was seen riding alone through the cornfield in pursuit of the armed fugitives. He captured an enemy mount, and still holds the horse and saddle as trophies.*[213]

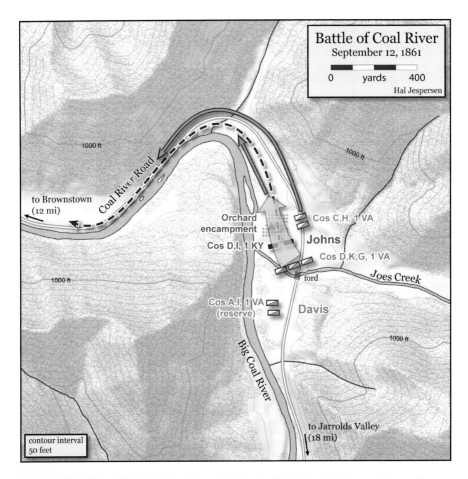

Battle of Coal River. The Rebel cavalry under Lucius Davis launched a surprise attack on a Union raiding force camped at Joes Creek. *Author's collection.*

Captains Caskie and McGruder's companies largely remained in reserve with Davis and did not reach the battlefield until the affair had nearly ended. Davis, in his report of the action, credited Clarkson for his direction of the victory. It was an excited moment—probably the most triumphant that the Confederate cavalry arm had yet known in the mountains, if not the war. A "private in Capt. Pate's company, had the breech of his gun shattered by a Dutchman Blue, whom he killed. His gun was at his shoulder, and both shot about the same time."[214] Private James H. Loughborough, of Caskie's Rangers, "overtook and captured a number of prisoners."[215]

Incidents of courage, gallantry and daring abounded, especially in Rosser's company, who "cut up the enemy so quickly that upon their arrival at Toney's [the other companies] had nothing to do but to pursue the scattered fugitives."

> *Private [James P.] Harrison, after killing his man, and finding his carbine unfit for further use, seized the man's musket and dashed alone in the midst of the enemy, receiving a shot through his jacket.*
>
> *Private William [H.] Pannell, to obtain a better sight of the enemy, and to shoot with greater accuracy, leaped upon the fence in the most dangerous of the conflict.*
>
> *Private Wiley Williams, expecting to be ordered on a farther pursuit, while the balls were flying thick around him, deliberately dismounted and nailed a shoe on his horse.*
>
> *Private [Walter A.] Bernard, by great presence of mind, by quickly inclining his head side-ways, saved his life, receiving a slight abrasion of the skin, on his neck, from a ball shot by a man, whom he instantly shot down.*
>
> *Sergeant Wm. Powell, Privates Willis Otey and James P. Lovell had their horses shot—Powell's dangerously. Sergeants Powell, Turner, and Wood, and Privates [John] J.P. Turner, [Bruce] B.A. James, [James] J.L. Dickinson, John Brooks, [Gabriel] G.T. Mattox, [E.H.] Poindexter, and H.S. Wright [Caskie's Rangers], may be favorably noticed for their success in killing and capturing the enemy.*[216]

Some Federal soldiers escaped up Short Creek and over Lens Creek Mountain. Other Federals, in the belief that the Confederates were at their heels, escaped to Peytona.[217] The casualties of this severely fought battle are variously given. Colonel Davis reported, at the highest reckoning, sixty Union soldiers killed, fifty wounded and forty-nine taken prisoner, "including stragglers."[218] The *Richmond Examiner* reported: "The fruits of this short but decisive affair were over fifty killed and wounded, forty-nine prisoners, sixty-one beeves, a large amount of arms, ammunition, etc."[219] Though Davis overestimated the number of Union killed and wounded, this defeat was nevertheless stunning for the Federals because the equivalent of a company was captured.

When he learned of the battle, Union private Francis G. Hale, Company F, Thirty-fourth Ohio Infantry, at Brownstown, attested in his diary:[220]

> *Co. I had there captaine takeing prisners and 30 sme odd more men with him they first Kentucky do not know what to do they went out on a scirmish after*

some cattle and got them in eight miles of camp when a lot of cavelry lit on them and killed 3 and took about forty prisners the boy told me they fit like the Devil but they had to go they was scatered so they would not do nothing hardly but they killed more secech then the secech killed and took of them.[221]

The *Cincinnati Daily Press* reported five Union soldiers killed, six wounded and forty captured.

The following is a list of the killed, wounded and prisoners on our side:
Thomas VanFleet, Newport, Ky, killed;
John Bolles, Newport, Ky, killed;
James Lawrence, Newport, Ky, killed;
Frank Webber, Newport, Ky, killed.
The latter is a brother of our informant.
Sergeant Robinson, Cincinnati, killed.
Morris Quinlan, of Newport, wounded in the leg; ---- Potter shot through the arm; Frederick Artz wounded twice in the leg; ---- Harber shot through the shoulder. The foregoing belong to Company I.
Company D lost twenty-two men, and had two wounded.
Captain Gibbs and Corporal Tittle, of Company I, and Lieutenant Fearron were taken prisoners. Besides the above, fifteen men of Company I were taken prisoners.
Our men lost their cattle, but succeeded in bringing away eight horses.[222]

The captured included Captain Cox, taken prisoner some distance in the rear of his men after their retreat.[223] One Confederate official remarked to President Jefferson Davis about the Federal losses that "they are a part of the miscreant band which burned Boone Court-House." He added:

Through respect to those holy laws which we are not at liberty to disobey, no matter how vile their conduct, we must extend towards our enemies the benefit of Christian charity and forbearance; but truly our people have been sorely tempted, and it is no less a matter of astonishment than of rejoicing that they have so constantly manifested that noble characteristic of the brave-mercy towards the fallen.[224]

The several dozen Federal soldiers who were captured—"a motley set of miserable looking scoundrels" and "cut-throat looking fellows"—were sent to Libby Prison at Richmond, where they suffered terribly.[225] During

Libby Prison was a Confederate prison in Richmond, Virginia. It gained an infamous reputation for the overcrowded and harsh conditions under which Union prisoners were kept, including sixty-three Union soldiers and Boone militia captured in the Coal River Valley in September 1861. *Library of Congress.*

his captivity as a prisoner of war through June 1863, when he was finally exchanged, Captain Cox behaved with conspicuous heroism caring for fellow prisoners.[226]

The Confederate victors found themselves with the entire train, some fifty to sixty horses and mules, government and private wagons and goods taken from different parties and being driven to the Federal camp, together with the freed political prisoners, including Pack's family and slaves. The *Cincinnati Daily Press* reported thirty-two Confederates killed.[227] However, according to Davis, the Confederates lost none killed, wounded or missing.[228] (In fact, Private Bernard of Rosser's company was slightly wounded.)[229] This can best be accounted for by the surprise and devastating effect on morale of the Confederate cavalry charge and sabers, the Rebel troopers scattering the unsuspecting Federal infantry and driving them in all directions.

The battle at Coal River on September 12, 1861, went little noticed in the North. This is primarily because, as the Confederate cavalry had begun their bold and difficult descent on Big Coal, General Floyd, on September 10, had defeated General Rosecrans at Carnifex Ferry, and this larger event in western Virginia and the war in general commanded the greater public attention of the nation (and, later, Civil War history). Meanwhile, for the Rebels, the Battle of Coal River came at a time when its effect on morale was most needed, after a long series of humiliating Confederate reverses in western Virginia. The battlefield followed the northern shore for several miles and fell within the Peytona district of Big Coal country, and for this reason, reports speak variously of the event as the Battle of Peytona instead of Toney's Creek, Joes Creek or Coal River, as it is also known.

Coal River was one of the first dramatic cavalry actions of the war anywhere, and its news excited attention in the South, especially in Richmond. The truth would appear to be that, while the Battle of Coal River avenged the burning of Boone Court House, the outcome equally created much embarrassment and indignation in the Union camp. When the panic-stricken survivors of the battle reached Brownstown with accounts of the disaster that had befallen the Federal raiders along the banks of the Big Coal, General Cox immediately sent two Federal infantry regiments the next day to find and attack the Rebel force.[230]

However, Colonel Davis, for his part, had been compelled to decide whether he should continue on his way, cross Short Creek and attack the Federal post at Peytona; make for the safety of Confederate lines; or rush down Lens Creek and attempt to capture the Federal base at Charleston or ride down Coal to attack Coalsmouth. Any of these accomplishments would be a considerable prize, and such a prospect was attractive, but Davis declined. He stopped short of attempting to reap the full success that appeared in the Confederates' grasp as the result of the brilliant fighting they had done.

The intention of hurrying on to Charleston…burning the steamboats, and by a rapid march returning with prisoners and booty, had to be abandoned, as our horses were found to be unfit for another rapid march.[231]

Not waiting for the Federal troops' arrival, the Confederate cavalry fell back to the upper Marshes of Coal (Glen Daniel-Fairdale). Confederate lieutenant Julius G. Tucker, with thirty men of the Jackson Rangers of Phelps' company, remained behind on the Big Coal as a rearguard to cover the Confederate withdrawal and, on September 13, captured several horses from Union men in the area.[232] In retaliation for supporting the South, the Federal force dispatched by General Cox scoured the Big Coal River Valley for several days, taking many political prisoners among the civilian population. Union Private Hale, at Brownstown, noted in his diary that the haul from Coal River yielded "35 secech broght in…as prisners."[233]

In addition, Davis reported that the Federals, "in a rage…fired the buildings at Toney's Creek & committed many outrages" before returning to Brownstown.[234] The Toney family homestead was especially targeted. At least a half dozen Toneys served in the Confederate army in Company I, Twenty-second Virginia Infantry Regiment, including its commander, Captain John P. Toney.[235] The "Yankee sympathizers" in the area, the Peytona Home Guards, raided the property and attempted to steal the Toney livestock and set the house on fire. However, the attack was "beaten off by kin and neighbors," the fire extinguished and the family rescued.[236]

The Battle of Coal River caused great excitement throughout the South. Lauding the victory of the Confederate cavalry, Dr. Benjamin Williams, assistant surgeon of the First Virginia Cavalry Regiment, said of the fight: "The fight at 'Toney's' will ever be recollected by those who won its laurels, or participated in its toils and hardships. The length, dangers, and rapidity of the march, and the boldness of the men, scarcely find a parallel in the pages of history."[237]

Chapter 4

POND FORK

As was tradition at the time, Civil War forts generally were named after the area where the fort was located or to honor their commanders. Or they were named after generals. To the best of current records, we do not know exactly what the Union militia called their small fort at Walnut Gap near the line separating Boone and Wyoming Counties other than probably "Camp Boone"—in defiance of the Rebel camp of the same name at Boone Court House. The fortifications were the work of Reverend William Walker Sr., along with his son-in-law Floyd Cooke and others in the summer of 1861. A staunch supporter of the Union cause and an abolitionist, Walker lived with his family at Bald Knob near the Workman settlement across Laurel Fork, just above Turkey Ridge. He reportedly cast the only vote for Abraham Lincoln in Boone County in 1860.[238] His son, Captain William Walker Jr., organized and commanded a Union militia company in the Boone-Wyoming area attached to the 190th Virginia Militia Regiment (Wyoming).

"The neighborhood is an unsound one," reported the Confederate commissioner who represented the area in the Virginia legislature.

> *A company was formed there that placed obstructions in the road and fortified themselves; attempted to take possession of mountain passes on the head of Pond Fork of Little Coal River, the most direct route to East Tennessee; and threatened to burn the town of Oceana.*[239]

The situation was known and appreciated by the military authorities of both the North and South, who expected to use these routes. When the Pond Fork men fortified themselves for protection against horse thieves and the Confederate militia who were assembling downstream at Boone Court House, they chose the site on the hills overlooking Skin Fork, a tributary creek of the Pond Fork of the Little Coal River, about twenty-seven miles southeast of Boone Court House. It was a high place in the area where they could look down on any enemy approaching and impede such possibility. This was home country to the men, who moved with ease along the creeks and paths. As they saw it, or hoped, a company of men stationed at the fort would be able to see up and down the valley and watch for hostile forces.

Thus, the fort likely got its name from Walker. Certainly, it was associated with him. Whether it was called Walker's Fort, Fort Walker, Camp Walker, simply Camp Boone or some other name (Cooke's fort or camp), the Union militia who were based there, all members of the Pond Fork detachment of the Peytona Home Guards company, had no way of knowing that the place they had selected for their camp, above the floor of the Pond Fork Valley, was about to be attacked and that most of them would shortly be captured. Nor could they know that the man responsible for their fate was a fellow Boone County neighbor—Henry Clay Pate.

It may be said that the arrival of Henry Clay Pate in September 1861 was a significant factor for the Confederates in the Coal River Valley. First, it augmented the Rebel militia with an organized fighting force, a seasoned, well-mounted and equipped cavalry company of about thirty troopers led by a smartly uniformed local personality. In the circumstances—the Rebels fearing a Unionist uprising and invasion by the Federals from the Kanawha Valley—Pate's arrival seemed heaven sent. He was exactly the type of man needed to leaven and give esprit to the Rebels. He was a talented cavalry leader who adopted the shock tactics of charging home at the gallop sword in hand. He led daring, whirlwind rides and attacks with enthusiasm and ferocity.

Born in 1832 in Bedford County, Virginia, Pate was named for the American statesman Henry Clay. His father, Edward Pate, had served in the War of 1812 and the Virginia legislature. Henry studied law (1848–50) at the University of Virginia, but the financial requirements of his father's establishment of the Coal River Navigation Company at Peytona required him to discontinue his studies. He went to live with his parents at Mouth of Short Creek and assisted his father and elder brother, William, in establishing the enterprise. Discontented with the nation's politics, he went for a time to Louisville, where he wrote for

Confederate captain Henry C. Pate, commander, Pate's Rangers, First Regiment, Wise's Legion Cavalry, Virginia Cavalry. Pate, whose family lived at Mouth of Short Creek (Racine) in Boone County, fought with his company at Coal River and Pond Fork. *West Virginia State Archives.*

newspapers and resumed studying law. He moved to Cincinnati in 1851 and wrote a book criticizing Virginia's decline among the American states and bought a newspaper that he sold in 1855.

Moving to Kansas he joined the pro-slavery movement, establishing another newspaper and practicing law. Pate was present when Lawrence, Kansas, was sacked and burned. After the murders of pro-slavery settlers at Pottawatomie by militant abolitionists led by John Brown in 1856, Pate and other pro-slavery militants battled with Brown and his men in the Battle of Black Jack, where Pate's force was defeated. He returned frequently to Virginia to raise funds to help finance the Kansas and Missouri pro-slavery movement. He moved to Petersburg, Virginia, in 1860 and published a pro-secessionist newspaper. When the war came, Pate sold the paper and recruited a cavalry company for service with Wise's Legion in western Virginia.

Therefore, Henry Clay Pate, twenty-nine years old, was already a veteran commander. On his arrival in the western Virginia mountains in the summer of 1861, the company was mustered into Wise's Legion and served largely on picket duty and scouting. Pate was a man of reckless courage, headstrong and flamboyant. There was no doubt about his lust for fame and that he wanted to make a name for himself. His exploits in the prewar Kansas strife and his all in for the South temperance made him a living terror to Unionists in the mountains.

Meanwhile, after the Battle of Coal River five days earlier (September 12), the Confederate cavalry under Davis had withdrawn to the Marshes of Coal (present-day Glen Daniel-Fairdale), where they let their horses graze and rest after the engagement. The Confederate victory proved that Cox's Coal River Valley flank was vulnerable. The Federal menace on the Big Coal River line temporarily bloodied, the thoughts of Pate and his fellow Confederates turned to retribution for the Federal depredations at Boone Court House and Toney's Creek. From the Marshes, the Confederates laid their plans for the elimination of the Federal fort at Pond Fork that controlled the important mountain passes at the head of Pond Fork of Little Coal River.

Indeed, after the battle at Boone Court House, seemingly one idea directed the thinking of the Confederates in southwestern Virginia: the Rebels openly wanted vengeance. And swiftly after Coal River, here was another opportunity, and they pressed on determinedly toward achieving it. The small fort at Pond Fork swung the military advantage in the area in favor of the Federals, who were actively recruiting companies for a new regiment of Virginia volunteers loyal to the Union.

> *There is evidence that some of the entrenched men were members of the Peytona Home Guards, and were at Boone Court House during the fighting, but there is no evidence that any of them actually applied the torches to the building. In fact, one pensioner mentioned the Home Guards had removed their records from the courthouse before it was destroyed.*[240]

The Confederate authorities considered the Union company "a most dangerous and treasonable organization…[that if] not broken up it may give the Federal army most important aid." The *Staunton Spectator* reported: "These fellows are said to be the party who burned Boone Court-House, and have been committing various depredations in the county."[241] Colonel Davis ordered Confederate captains Pate and Caskie's companies into northern Wyoming and southern Boone counties specifically for the purpose of breaking up this "den of tories."[242] Capturing William Walker Jr., "who is an open and avowed Tory, and is doing us much harm," was part of the Confederate plan.[243] In addition, the Confederates wanted to capture William Workman and Floyd Cooke, who were the leaders in the Union Home Guard movement on the Pond Fork and had been with the Federal force that burned Boone Court House.[244]

Pate, of course, knew Boone County well since his family had lived there for more than a decade. Caskie had operated throughout the Kanawha Valley region during the summer and with the Rebel militia in Raleigh, Fayette and Mercer Counties.[245] By this time, Caskie's Rangers reportedly had already "done more marching and stood more fatigue and hardship than any other company in the war." They had been "the last to evacuate Charleston, and covered Wise's withdrawal to Gauley Bridge. In Kanawha Valley, Caskie's Rangers are well known for their exploits and daring acts against the enemy."[246]

After a few days resting at the Marshes, Pate and Caskie's companies, about sixty troopers, detached and struck for southern Boone on September 16. Fired by the exploits of Clarkson and Rosser at Coal River, their objective was the Union company based at Skin Fork, about twenty miles from the Marshes of Coal. The Skin Fork's mouth was about a half mile southeast of the little settlement of Pond Fork, named after the river that flowed past. Near there, the Union militia had built their "formidable breastwork in that neighborhood."

The Union redoubt is described piecemeal in the *Official Records*. Floyd Cooke gave an account of the fortifications as follows: "Trees had been cut across the road and…some brush thrown up on the side of the mountain which were many logs and stones in it." Seemingly, it was a small earthwork dug into the mountainside with a bastioned front. In front of this heap of dirt, reinforced plentifully with rocks and boulders, was the valley floor for a distance of about a quarter mile. In front, the dense forest had been felled, thus forming a labyrinth of tangled timber difficult to penetrate.[247]

Early the next day, Pate launched the attack that became known as the Battle of Pond Fork. It was a spectacle of complete surprise. The Confederate raiders descended on the area undiscovered, and "on the morning of the 17th, Capt. Pate's company of Mounted Rangers assailed the entrenched camp." The fifty or more Union militia were surprised while forming. They saw the Rebel cavalry before they were upon the fort and "made no resistance, with the exception of firing one gun, and took to their heels for safety." The Confederates charged with pistols and drawn sabers. The conflict within the breastworks lasted only briefly before the Union garrison was overwhelmed. Thus, within a matter of minutes of launching the assault, the rout was complete.

It was bedlam as men ran about in all directions and fled up the side of the mountain as the Confederates stormed over the entrenchments and took the Union fort. After the skirmish was over, Captain Pate's company caught and arrested some of the men and charged them with treason against the Confederate states. Among the men captured was Captain Peter Miller, a Union army recruiting agent who had been raising and organizing volunteers for Federal service in the area. Miller had formed the troops into a company and was the senior officer present. Pate reported that "Miller attempted to

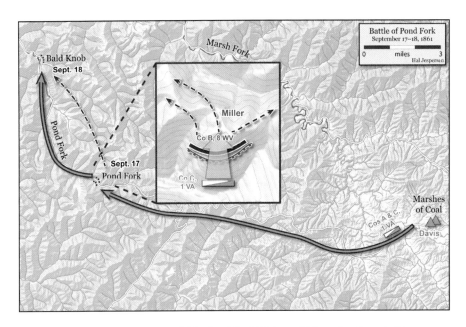

Battle of Pond Fork. A company of fifty Pond Fork Union militia under Captain Peter Miller was attacked in its fort and dispersed by a force of Confederates under Captain Henry C. Pate. *Author's collection.*

escape up a mountain and was shot while making this attempt." He was "captured, and a valuable pistol taken from him, [and] a very valuable black horse…A quantity of letter paper and envelopes were found on his person."[248]

In the meantime, while Pate's Rangers were taking their prisoners and ransacking the Union fort, Captain Caskie and his company of mounted rangers raided the upper Pond Fork neighborhoods nearby. They rounded up forty-seven head of cattle. It seems that the Confederates remained in the area that night, camping at the fort. Before departing, Pate burned the Union camp and everything in it that could not be carried off. The next day, September 18, he struck out for Bald Knob, about five miles away.

There, the Union militia attempted to regroup at the homestead of Amos Workman, William Workman's brother and one of the leaders of the Union militia. "Workman's place" was the family settlement across Laurel Fork, above Turkey Ridge at Bald Knob. The militia resisted briefly but again were put to flight, and more of them were captured. During their raid, the Rebels took seventeen Union militia as prisoners. Pate sent out parties in several directions in the Bald Knob area, and they torched the houses of Union militia members, including those of Workman and Floyd Cooke and his eighteen-year-old son, George Cook. (Floyd was the last in his line to spell his surname as Cooke.)

The Confederates released three of the prisoners, including the elderly Reverend William Walker Sr. and two young boys, and sent the remaining fourteen captives to Richmond. Militia records indicate that Private Samuel B. McNeely, a member of the Workman clan, was also captured during this time.[249]

> *Among those arrested were: William Workman; Floyd and George Cook; Floyd, Simeon, Jackson, and Irvin Jarrell, and Harrison Wall. Three of the Jarrells, Simeon, Jackson and Irvin died in Libby Prison during their confinement. Floyd and George Cook were held in the Richmond prison for 18 months before being released in February 1863. They returned home to Boone County and found their home destroyed. Mary (Walker) Cooke, Floyd's wife (George's mother), died September 21, 1861, her death no doubt caused by her husband's arrest and the destruction of their home. Left behind were 8 children, 6 of whom were under 10 years of age.[250]*

In addition, Joseph Workman, the father of William Workman and patriarch of the Workman clan, was also taken prisoner:

> [Workman was] *at least seventy-five years old, poorly clad, and the very picture of forlorn despair. What was this poor old creature's offense? It had been said that in his little old farmhouse, up among the mountains of Western Virginia, where he had lived quietly for more than half a century, protected in all his rights, he had rehearsed to his children and grandchildren, year after year, with all the rapture of his youthful zeal, the story of his honorable service in the defense of his country during the war of 1812. Now, in his declining years, he had dared to say that he still loved the grand old flag, and could not and would not betray it. For this offense, he had been arrested and taken several hundred miles to Richmond, as a prisoner of war. He was not willing to renounce in his old age the government which had given him protection and support, and which his long life had taught him to revere. Grand, noble, patriotic old soul!*[251]

The Confederate victories in the Battles of Coal River and Pond Fork avenged the burning of Boone Court House. However, even together they did not break the Federal control over the Coal River Valley or lead to its recovery by the Confederacy. Though tactical victories of the first order, strategically the outcome set a pall of fear on both sides in the region. The results blazoned the startling truth that neither the Federal army in the Kanawha Valley nor the Union Home Guard companies at Peytona, Mud River and Pond Fork could protect homes and property. And when the Confederates withdrew after these successes because they lacked the strength to stay, it indicated that "the South could not establish her Confederacy" in the region, as a Coal River Valley resident astutely observed in his diary.[252]

In fact, there were to be many ups and downs throughout the region for both sides as the war dragged on for another three and half years, but never again was Confederate prestige as high throughout the Coal River Valley as it was after the Battles of Coal River and Pond Fork. Though little noticed at the time, the latter action marked the summit of Confederate success in the region. In the end, the significance of the fight at Pond Fork, especially, lay more in what it wrought than in what it achieved. The tide of Federal setbacks was about to turn. Just over a week later, another engagement would break the back of Confederate fortunes in the region. Thus was precipitated the Battle of Kanawha Gap, the decisive engagement of this brief but important series of actions in and around the Coal River Valley.

Chapter 5

KANAWHA GAP

In the 1861 summer campaign in southwestern Virginia, Colonel James Ward Davis served on the staff of General Wise as an aide-de-camp. As he was an able administrator, Wise sent him to take charge of organizing the militia in the largely pro-Confederate counties of Wyoming, Logan and Boone. Colonel Davis at once went to work to muster and organize the 190th (Wyoming), 187th (Boone) and 129th (Logan and Nicholas) regiments of Virginia state militia for service with Wise. Thereafter, events moved rapidly.

First, in answer to the muster in Boone County of the 187th Regiment, a Federal force sacked and burned rebellious Boone Court House (September 1). Colonel Ezekiel Miller withdrew his Southern militia companies to Logan Court House. On September 12, the Confederates responded with startling success. A hot engagement was fought from Joes Creek to the mouth of Toney's Creek on the Big Coal River in which a battalion of Rebel cavalry dispersed a Federal raiding force. Contact was made again between the armies of the North and South when Confederate cavalry raided and overcame a Union militia company in their fortifications at Pond Fork (September 17).

Appreciating that the Federals in the Kanawha Valley were overextended and emboldened by their victories at Coal River and Pond Fork, the Confederates were anxious that the Coal River Valley be re-conquered. General Floyd detested the idea of falling back from southwestern Virginia until winter prevented a Federal advance south. Further, his army was so badly found that he was compelled to look for a well-stocked area in which to winter his troops in southwestern Virginia. He would write:

I still adhere to my original purpose of wintering near Logan Court-House…Those who know the topography of the country from the map alone cannot perceive without explanation its complete security. If the enemy have 15,000 troops so near to that place as Charleston, what, they will ask, is to prevent them from marching over there after communications have been cut off with Eastern Virginia by the weather, breaking up my winter quarters, and perhaps capturing my whole command. I answer, the maps do not show that between Charlestown and Logan Court-House there are two immense chains of mountains, and that the passes through those mountains are among the most easily-defended localities on the continent. It is ground with which I am perfectly familiar, and with the troops now under me I can safely guarantee my defense against twice the force which the enemy can by any contrivance bring against me.

The question of security may be laid aside. It remains to consider the more difficult matter of supplies at a point so remote from the center of the State. Ammunition and the small commissary stores, such as candles, sugar, coffee, and clothing, would be brought by the Virginia and Tennessee road to a station within 130 miles of my camp. The roads from that point to Logan are of course bad, but I can have them soon put in sufficient repair for my purposes. Forage in sufficient quantities for all my cattle I do not hope to obtain around my proposed camp, and therefore, after establishing myself, I should send away all the horses and mules that I do not absolutely need to Tazewell, where their wants can be fully met. It rests to ascertain whether I can get enough meat and meal in the country for my men. I think I can, but I cannot say so with perfect assurance till I have myself examined the present resources of those counties; but the advantages to be gained by establishing my quarters in that region are so great, that I am determined, unless prevented by your orders, to make the experiment. My plan at present is to try for some weeks what I can do against the enemy's army. Then I will go to Logan, hut my troops, stockade my camp, fortify the approaches, repair the roads, and ascertain the capability of the country to support my army. If it is sufficient to carry us through the winter without suffering at all, I shall remain till the spring, unless I should see a good chance for a blow during the winter; but if the country has been too much exhausted by the war and the enemy, I will at least stay there till the end of November, up to which time there can be no difficulty, and then march my men up to the Lynchburg and Tennessee road.[253]

Floyd thus had a clear concept of how the Boone-Logan region might serve as the place for his army's winter cantonment and jumping-off point in 1862. The Unionists at Pond Fork and Bald Knob had been burned out, and most of the region's inhabitants sympathized with the South. Floyd thought he could supply his forces there, gather recruits and draw the Union army deeper into the mountains and farther away from Richmond. In the spring, the Confederates would take back and hold Boone Court House, then reduce the troublesome Unionist stronghold at Peytona and lastly take or destroy Brownstown on the Kanawha River, the base for Federal operations in the Coal River Valley. At that point, the Confederates would be between Gauley Bridge and Charleston,

Confederate brigadier general John B. Floyd commanded the Army of the Kanawha and Department of Western Virginia and anticipated making the Guyandotte and Coal River Valleys the site of his army's winter camp. *Library of Congress.*

splitting the Federal army in the Kanawha Valley. So Floyd imagined.

Colonel James Ward Davis, in command of the Confederate militia operating in this region where Floyd was the commander, was directed to concentrate his troops and cavalry reinforcements sent to him on the Guyandotte River line, south and west of the Little Coal River. "Weakened by manpower drained off into the regular service, the county's 129th Militia Regiment was no longer effective."[254] Davis had reorganized the Confederates at Logan Court House, building up his force from the Boone and Logan militia veterans of Boone Court House, including the Black Striped Company. Within a few weeks, he succeeded in raising their combined strengths to 225 men. After the fall of Boone Court House and their retreat to Logan Court House, Chapmanville was the logical point for concentration of the defeated Confederate forces. Located within the elbow bend of the Guyandotte River, Chapmanville was at the junction of two important roads: the Boone–Logan road and the Logan–Barboursville road. Chapmanville was about a twenty-one-mile march southeast of Boone Court House. Davis proceeded to Chapmanville with the aim of attacking and breaking up the Union militia at Peytona.

While Davis was preparing for the Confederate counteroffensive, General Cox, the imaginative strategist, was not idle. Having razed Boone Court House and then lost two companies ignominiously at Coal River and Pond Fork, Cox determined to respond boldly. Learning that the Rebels were gathering in force, supported by cavalry, Cox in response forthwith directed Colonel Guthrie to organize and send a Union force on a forced march to oppose and disperse the Confederates that his scouts reported were preparing to advance on Peytona.

Guthrie selected the Thirty-fourth Ohio Infantry Regiment's commander, Colonel Abraham S. Piatt, to command the expedition. The organization of the Federal force from Cox's Kanawha Brigade at Piatt's disposal was as follows:

First Kentucky Infantry Regiment, Lieutenant Colonel David Enyart

Company A, Captain Wheeler
Company H, Captain Frank P. Cahill
Company J, Captain Andrew J. Hogan

Thirty-fourth Ohio Infantry Regiment

Companies A, Captain Thomas W. Rathbone
Company B, Captain Oliver P. Evans
Company C, Captain Austin C. Miller
Company H, Captain Herman C. Evans
Company I, Captain James A. Anderson
Company F, Captain Samuel R.S. West

First Kentucky Light Artillery

Simmonds' Battery, Captain Seth J. Simmonds[255]

To these units must be added the four Union Home Guard companies at Peytona numbering about two hundred men. Together this made a grand total of over one thousand troops.

Union soldier of the Thirty-fourth Ohio Infantry Regiment. *Library of Congress.*

Colonel Piatt, forty years old, was a wealthy farmer and newspaper owner from southern Ohio who had attended what is now Xavier University. His wife had died in April 1861, and he threw himself into raising two regiments of volunteers for Federal service. On September 1, Piatt and the Thirty-fourth Ohio Infantry Regiment moved to camp at Cincinnati and from there to western Virginia. The Federals took up their line of march from Brownstown early on September 23. For the Thirty-fourth Ohio, three weeks fresh from mustering in Ohio, this was their first outing.

The troops were uniformed in Zouave (zoo-ahh-vah) dress in the French North African style—a short, dark blue jacket trimmed with red edges; sky blue trousers with a red double stripe and tucked into russet leather leggings;

and a fez like those worn in the Ottoman armies. The Thirty-fourth was one of two Ohio regiments so attired. They were called the Piatt Zouaves, after the colonel who had raised the regiment, and also the First Ohio Zouaves.

A participant who accompanied the force reported: "The object of the expedition was to attack a body of rebels said to be congregated there [at Peytona], and to avenge the loss of our men, which occurred in what is known here as the 'John's Expedition' [Battle of Coal River, September 12]."[256]

Colonels Piatt and Enyart's forces moved in column until they reached the Big Coal River at Mouth of Short Creek. Here, the Federals were joined by the two hundred Union militia of the Peytona Home Guards.

> *On reaching Peytona, it was found that the enemy had fled—part of them having gone to Logan, forty miles distant, and part to Raleigh, distant eighty-five miles. It was determined to pursue them, so our force was divided—the Zouaves taking the road to Logan, the Kentuckians that to Raleigh.*[257]

To mislead the Confederates, then, Enyart took a sizeable force of about 250 troops of the First Kentucky Infantry Regiment, the 200 Home Guards and a section of the light artillery up the Big Coal River into Raleigh County. It was a total of about 500 men. The long and arduous sixty-mile march they underwent was epic. In fierce storms, they crossed mountains, fast-flowing rivers and treacherous marshes. As Captain Hogan, commanding Company J, First Kentucky, reported:

> *On the evening of the second day out, our bread, coffee, and sugar were entirely exhausted. On the fourth day, (having subsisted on half-cooked beef alone for nearly 36 hours,) we arrived at a point ten miles from Raleigh. Here a terrific storm overtook us, and a fierce rain commenced pouring down, lasting without cessation for forty-five hours. Having no tents, and many of us no blankets, we were completely exposed to the storm, sleeping on the wet grass at night, and marching through mud and rain during the day. On the morning of the fifth day we entered Raleigh, (the rain still falling in torrents,) just in time to see the rear guard of the enemy retreating in double quick step from the town. As they were on horseback and we were on foot, pursuit was useless, so we contented ourselves with giving them a parting volley, which "settled the hash" of one Secessionist, at least.*
>
> *Here we were, then, nearly one hundred miles from Charleston, and without provisions. There were none to be had at Raleigh, as the enemy had literally devoured everything in the country for miles around the town.*

In this dilemma it was determined to push forward to Camp Gauley, but on advancing a few miles, it was found that the heavy rains of the two preceding days had caused an immense rise in the streams crossing the road, and had swept away the bridges. The roads were consequently impassable. We were compelled to turn back.

It was then resolved to effect a junction with the Zouaves, at Wyoming. Our troops commenced a countermarch for this purpose, but after a hard tramp of over twelve miles in that direction, "we came to a bridge which we couldn't get across," as it had been totally carried off by the freshet. No other alternative was left but to retrace our steps down Coal River. The men had by this time been without food for over twenty-four hours, so a halt was called, a couple of old cows were captured, killed and eaten, half cooked. After a brief rest we started again, but our progress was speedily checked by the fearful rise in Coal River; and it being now nearly dark, we lay down in the wet and mud, and worn out with fatigue, we soon fell into a heavy sleep.

With the break of day we were aroused, and, the river being still impassable, we concluded to take to the mountains, leaving the wagons behind in charge of Capt. Wheeler's company, to be brought in as soon as the stream fell (This duty the Captain has since nobly performed.) This course was necessary, inasmuch as the river was not only impassable, but had completely washed away all traces of the road along the way…

Our force, numbering about two hundred and fifty men, now commenced their weary march over the mountains, and in the afternoon reached the Clear Fork of Coal. Here, the road having been entirely washed away, they took the bed of the river as the route, and for two whole days marched up to their waist in water through the stream. At night, wet and weary, the men threw themselves on the grass; and slept as soundly as if on feather beds. So much for the result of fatigue. On the ninth day the troops reached Camp Enyart, and on the tenth entered Charleston, having accomplished a march of over two hundred and ten miles in nine days, during seven of which they were almost entirely out of food. As an evidence of the endurance of our men, it may be mentioned that but two of them "gave out" during the march.

Capt. Cahill had a narrow escape for his life. He was crossing a bridge of logs, on horseback, when the structure commenced floating away. The horse became frightened and kicked the logs apart, precipitating himself and rider into the stream, at this point some twelve feet deep. The struggling of the animal rendered the Captain's position extremely critical. Fortunately, both were rescued unhurt.[258]

In this manner, the Union force took Raleigh Court House on September 27 after the Rebel cavalry who defended the place withdrew without a fight.

Col. Enyart did not meet the enemy in force at any place, but his men did meet and ford swollen rivers, and marched on short rations, and were anxious to meet with the running enemy of old Virginia. Col. Enyart did not join Col. Piatt until they met on the Kanawha, on their return.[259]

The aftereffects of Enyart's arduous march up Big Coal to Raleigh Court House were significant, revealing the region's vulnerability to a determined advance of Federal forces. Thereafter, in the fall, troops under General Cox eventually occupied Fayette Court House and pressed farther southward. The Confederates stubbornly disputed the advance at Raleigh Court House and a ford near the junction of Piney River and Beaver Creek. There, the advancing Federals and defending Confederates fought a sharp skirmish in which Union artillery shelled the town. The Confederates were forced to withdraw, and the Federal troops occupied Raleigh Court House.

After the first occupation by Union forces, the government of Raleigh County ceased to function for the remainder of the war. The absence of an effective government, the political divisions and the movements of Union and Confederate armies through 1862 sparked a large level of violence between erstwhile neighbors in the Coal and New River Valleys. After 1863, Union forces remained in the region fighting Confederate sympathizers known as "Bushwhackers" until the conclusion of the war.[260]

Meanwhile, Piatt's command numbering about 560 men and a section of the light artillery proceeded to Boone Court House. Union private Charles A. Stough, Company E, Thirty-fourth Ohio Infantry, wrote: "In the evening about five o'clock, we arrived there. All that could be seen was the smoky walls of what was at one time a pretty village. We went on about a mile farther, and encamped for the night."[261]

The next day, after proceeding about sixteen miles, they came upon Confederate cavalry pickets serving as the advance guard of Colonel James Ward Davis' command.[262] When Piatt advanced to Boone Court House, Davis' cavalry discovered the movement. Davis ordered the cavalry to impede Piatt's advance and harass the Federals but to retire if the enemy reacted in force. The opposing forces first clashed at Washington Township (present-day Manila, U.S. Route 119) on the Trace Fork of Big Creek. They exchanged a brisk fire, and the Rebel cavalry retreated. After the cavalry was driven off, Piatt formed the Federal force in order of battle. Captain Ezra W. Clark, who served on the staff of Colonel Piatt as adjutant, led the advance guard of fifteen men forward along the road. Scouts were sent out on either side to meet and repulse the enemy pickets. For two hours, the Federals advanced, meeting the cavalry pickets of the enemy, exchanging shots with them incessantly and charging and driving them back for two miles. "At every turn of the road over the mountains," Piatt reported, "they would fire upon our advance men, wheel round, and gallop away."[263]

Private Stough, Company E, Thirty-fourth Ohio Infantry, wrote: "Every few minutes the fire was repeated, and so on for the distance of three miles, when they commenced firing on us from different parts of the hill. We kept on until the fire became so hot that the Colonel ordered skirmishers out on the right, when we again moved on up the hill, until we came up to what is called the Kanawa [sic] Gap."[264]

The Rebels were pursued down the Trace Fork Valley for three miles to a heavily forested mountainside. Piatt halted his entire force for a few moments. He rode forward to the skirmish line, drew up his glass and took observations of the ground to determine the prospects of an attack but could not ascertain the enemy's forces and position. In fact, the Rebels held a very strong position. They were posted in the mountain pass at Kanawha Gap, which they had blocked with felled trees as obstructions, and had infantry with skirmishers on the heights on every side. The Rebel position seemed impregnable, hidden in thick underbrush and woods and protected by large, craggy rocks, while the Union ranks would be exposed to galling crossfire. The Federals would be compelled to carry the gap by storm.

After he completed his observations, Piatt, determined the enemy was there to be assailed and to fulfill his mission, ordered the blue column forward. The Federal scouts moved with rapidity and enthusiasm, the main body moving up the narrow road under Lieutenant Colonel John T. Toland, an officer of devotion, natural ability and, as soon would be proved, distinguished courage. The Confederate fire continued to increase as shots were rapidly exchanged from the right and left with unseen enemy skirmishers until the Federals' advanced guard reached the main Confederate force about two miles northeast of Chapmanville, which lay beyond the gap.

The Confederate force was commanded by Colonel Davis, who had not been idle during the Federal advance from Peytona. He had collected in total his 225 men at Chapmanville, including about 50 cavalry sent to his aid by Floyd.[265] His troops were thinly spread in the entrenchments that

Site of the main fighting in the Battle of Kanawha Gap on September 25, 1861. This view is two miles northeast of Chapmanville, looking southward on U.S. Route 119. *Author's collection.*

had been rapidly constructed to meet the expected Union attack. The main defensive works were set on an elevated position commanding the road and the valley northward, as well as east and west. The mountain was steep and covered with thick woods and heavy undergrowth. Nature could not have made a stronger position, and this the Rebels fortified with breastworks of logs, brush, rocks and dirt. From their position, the Confederates could see almost all movement one thousand feet below, while they themselves were sheltered and concealed by the forested growth on the mountainsides. Davis' strategy, however much beyond his means to achieve, was sound in principle, as judged by how it had upset the Union army's operations in the Kanawha Valley and diverted a large force from otherwise supporting General Cox at Gauley Bridge.

Indeed, this was not Boone Court House three weeks earlier. Instead of panicking and running away as they had when Rook's Charge carried the Little Coal, Ward Davis' men coolly waited in their trench system and sent down a storm of fire that crumpled the Federal direct assault up the mountainside. The blue-clad infantry saw little but a line of flashing fire and smoke ahead as they advanced uphill. Private John A. Williams, Company F, Thirty-fourth Ohio Infantry, kept a diary of his time in the war and wrote of the opening of this sharp engagement:

> *Our advanced guard were attacked by the rebels under command by Colonel Davis—the fight now commenced. We were in a gap with high hills on*

either side; the Johnnies were on the hills volley after volley were poured into us. As brave men we returned the fire and drove the rebels who retreated into their breastworks. The Battle now commenced in earnest. The Rebs poured volley after volley into our ranks. We gave them the best we had…[266]

Then, to the Union force's astonishment, when the Federal column was about eighty yards from the enemy, it received another sudden and perfect volley of deadly musket fire on their right, revealing that the Rebels were also concealed in force in that direction. Clearly, there was nothing for the Federals to do other than respond with maneuvering in that direction, too. Company A, commanded by Captain Rathbone, was ordered to deploy as skirmishers to the right, up the side of the mountain, and, if possible, flank the enemy on their left. Company C, commanded by Captain Miller, was ordered to the right, up a similar mountain, to flank the enemy on their left. The zing of Minié balls whistled around that part of the column where Piatt and Toland were commanding, exposed in the open, and after the battle, two model 1841 Harpers Ferry "Mississippi" sharpshooter rifles were collected on the battlefield.

This kind of fight was kept up till we came suddenly upon their breastwork, immediately in line of our entire column. It was made on the side of a knoll, between two mountain sides, the road running between the mountain and knoll on our right, and a small ravine running between the knoll and the mountain on our left. The wily rebel commander had adroitly cut down the brush on the right, placing a force of one hundred men on the mountain top on our right, who raked our column from the front to the centre. This was to draw our attention from their breastworks. Our men naturally fired upon the rebels on their right, steadily advancing up the road, until within twenty feet of the enemy's works, when the rebels suddenly opened fire from their right, left, and centre.[267]

Meanwhile, Company I, commanded by Captain Anderson, was ordered directly up the ravine, on the left. In this position, Anderson drew the concentrated fire of the Rebels upon his company, who made use of the knowledge thus obtained by rapidly charging up the side of the mountain and bounding the enemy's breastworks. While this movement occurred, the center force moved directly up the road. With this disposition of the forces, Piatt routed the Confederates from their main position, driving them in confusion from their defenses. Anderson himself was the first to mount the

Rebel breastworks, his inexperienced men following their leader in the face of a terrible fire without flinching or confusion.

> *The order from Col. Piatt and Lieut.-Col. Toland, to flank right and left, was immediately responded to by the Zouaves with a hurrah, a Zouave yell, and a cry of "wood up" from Little Red; a dash by our boys upon the enemy's right, left, and centre; a fire from the enemy's breastworks, above which about three hundred rebel heads suddenly appeared, unknown by our men till that moment. They sent a perfect storm of bullets, over, under, and into our men.* [268]

As the Federals charged uphill, Davis' fire was so fast and fierce that the ranks of Union infantry, surprised, wavered for a moment to comprehend what had happened. The Confederates raked them with such fearful carnage that they contemplated falling back. Finally, after the ground was littered with Union dead and wounded, the Rebels began to give ground, and their fire slackened. As Anderson scaled the breastworks, Miller closed upon the left and Rathbone upon the right, his men crying, "Zouave!"—the main column moving up the road in double-quick—until they were brought to a temporary halt by obstructions that had been placed in the road by the enemy. Here, a final charge was ordered. Private Williams recorded in his diary: "The Battle now commenced in earnest. The Rebs poured volley after volley into our ranks. We gave them the best we had and a charge was ordered. You ought to have heard the yell of the zouaves. We charged the breast works and routed the rebels. The day was ours we were successful in our 1st Battle." [269]

As these maneuvers were taking place, the Union flanking force of about one hundred men made its way up the mountain's one-thousand-foot western slope. In the assault, the men had to climb huge boulders, cross deep ravines and go through dense thickets of brush and timber. The fight for the western breastworks lasted about ten minutes. The hastily thrown-up earthworks were no match for the numbers of Federal troops assigned the task of taking them. In the fighting, Davis received desperate wounds that appeared mortal—a thumb and finger shot off, right arm broken and a gunshot wound in the breast.

The last barrier broken, surrounded by a larger force and their leader gravely injured, Confederate morale collapsed. With blue-clad infantry nearing the summit and others turning their rear, the Rebels now had to retreat. They did so in a hurry. After a few shots were fired, the Rebels

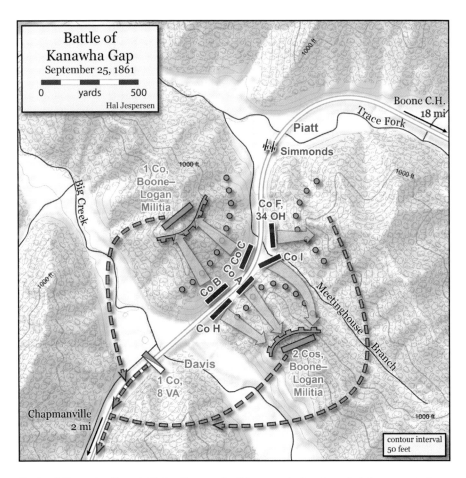

Battle of Kanawha Gap. A Union force under Piatt assaulted and carried the concealed Confederate positions defended by the Boone-Logan militia under Colonel James Ward Davis. *Author's collection.*

broke off their defense and discontinued the battle. They fled southward, leaving their dead, wounded, clothing, weapons, horses and prisoners taken in the trenches.

The main Confederate force made its escape by Rathbone's right, his company too far up the mountain to cut off their retreat.

> *Off they went, as though Satan, with all the imps of the infernal regions, was after them. We scoured the woods and hills all around us, and then returned to the road where we had the pleasure of seeing a flag of truce, which was taken to the Colonel with the bearer, who also stated that the rebels*

had retreated to Logan, (which is some twelve miles from Chapmanville).
Col. Davis was wounded and delivered himself up as a prisoner of war,
and requested medical aid.[270]

Captain West, commanding Company F, was detailed to scour the mountain on the west, on the left of the road. Captain Oliver P. Evans (Company B) was detailed to scour the west side of the mountain, on the right side of the road. Captain Herman Evans, commanding Company H, searched the east side of the mountain, on the left of the road. Owing to the thick forest and large rocks, it was difficult to scramble up the side of the mountain. Not knowing if the Rebels had withdrawn, Federal soldiers scaled the heights and found the Confederates gone from the summit. Each of these companies moved with dispatch, but the Rebels were so knowledgeable of the paths in the mountains that only two were captured on the heights. By this time, the Rebels on the mountain had withdrawn over the summit toward Chapmanville.

The battle was over. Among the objects captured was "a secesh flag twenty feet long, with FIFTEEN STARS."[271] First Lieutenant Ethan A. Brown, Company F, was among those who penetrated the enemy's lines and went over the Confederate works, in which he captured the colors.

We buried our three brave dead comrades that night, carried our wounded
to the house wherein the rebel colonel lay mortally wounded, desserted [sic]
by all his men but one. Our whole column finally marched into the little
town of Chapmanville, formerly headquarters of the enemy, and camped
for the night.[272]

Confederate private Samuel Smoot, of the Boone militia, participated in the fight. He wrote:

The Yankees numbered 700, and commenced the attack upon our troops—the
Logan militia—in a low gap between Guyandotte River and Big Creek,
where they were engaged in raising a temporary breastwork. Our troops
numbered 220, but there were only about 80 of them engaged in the fight.
They were commanded by Col. J.W. Davis of Greenbrier, a brave and
gallant officer, who was severely, but not dangerously wounded, in the arm
and breast. As soon as it became known that Col. Davis was wounded
the militia commenced a retreat. The commanding officer of the Lincoln
troops afterwards confessed to Col. Davis, who was taken prisoner, that at

Union soldier and fifer of the Thirty-fourth Ohio Infantry Regiment in Zouave uniform. Frank Leslie's Illustrated Newspaper, *November 8, 1862.*

the same moment a portion of the Yankees were running, and that one more round would have completely dispersed them. The loss of the Yankees by their own confession to Col. Davis, was forty killed and a number wounded. Among the former were four Union men, all of whom are represented by the Yankees to be most arrant thieves and cowards. Our loss was two killed and three or four slightly wounded, besides Col. Davis, whose valuable services are at present lost to the Confederacy, being paroled by the enemy.[273]

It is difficult to state accurately either the forces engaged at Kanawha Gap or the losses sustained by each side. The estimates of both the Union and Confederate sources vary considerably. Union private Stough wrote that the Rebel commander "says his force was only two hundred and fifty men, but the citizens and the muster rolls of the Regiment show over six hundred men. While our force all told was between five and six hundred."[274] It appears most probable that the Federals had almost 600 men on the field against a Confederate strength of about 225 men—the militia of Logan and Boone Counties and cavalry. (One estimate put the Confederate strength at "four hundred and fifty infantry, and fifty cavalry.")[275] The Federal losses were 3 killed and 9 wounded, 1 of whom later died.

It appears that the Confederate casualties were heavier, about sixty killed, wounded and captured combined—possibly more. The *Cincinnati Gazette* reported that "the enemy's loss was thirty killed and fifty wounded,"[276] while the *Cincinnati Commercial* stated the Confederates "left twenty-nine dead behind."[277] The *Staunton Spectator* reported "two killed and three or four slightly wounded." Pollard, in his *Southern History of the War*, reported two killed and two wounded.[278] A Union soldier reported about the Rebels: "Their loss is estimated at thirty killed, and a large number wounded. This is the report of some of their own men."[279] There is little doubt that the prisoners amounted to a large number as the Federal troops pursued them to Chapmanville and seemingly took dozens of stragglers in the area and camped for the night. The highest report estimated the Confederate losses at eighty killed, fifty wounded and forty-seven captured.[280] The *New York Times* reported that the Federals "surrounded and attacked the rebels at Chapmanville, and after a short engagement, completely routed them, killing sixty, and taking seventy prisoners. The rebels, in escaping, were intercepted by Col. PIATT who killed forty, and took a large number of prisoners."[281]

Thought to be mortally wounded by his troops, Confederate commander Davis had been left behind and was captured there with another wounded Southern man. Of the Federals in Company E, Private Stough wrote:

Union lieutenant colonel John T. Toland, deputy commander, Thirty-fourth Ohio Infantry Regiment. In battle for the first time at Kanawha Gap, Toland "demonstrated fully that he has courage to fight and ability to command." *Ohio State Archives.*

There is but one out of our Company who was hurt in the engagement: it is I. Bryant, whose arm was so fractured by a ball, that it had to be amputated. And being unable to be moved, we were compelled to leave him behind in care of a "secesh" doctor who took the oath of allegiance to the Union, and also said he would see Bryant well, and on his way home as soon as his arm was well enough for him to travel. [282]

After disengaging at Kanawha Gap, most of the bruised and battered Southern force got down to the Guyandotte, crossed to Chapmanville and stumbled slowly back to Logan Court House. Piatt's entire force followed and, on the night of September 25, went into bivouac in Chapmanville. The next day, their mission to attack and disperse the Confederates at Chapmanville accomplished, the Union troops began their return trek to the Kanawha Valley. The force was delayed at Boone Court House by the high waters of the Little Coal River. Union sergeant Albany Packham wrote that during "our homeward march—or, I should perhaps say homeward swim, for we were in the water two days and two nights…only half a cracker to each man was given out by our commissary."[283]

Union private Stough wrote:

We remained in Chapmanville that night and the following day. About four o'clock it commenced raining, and at two o'clock we were called out to start for home on account of being out of provisions. We started amid rain and mud, and marched all day without a mouthful to eat, until four o'clock in the afternoon, by which time we were at Cole [sic] River, and could not ford it, as it had been swollen so by the rain, which still came beating down, as though the very heavens were open, making our prospects very good for remaining at this place for two or three days. Piatt was at the head of the column, when it arrived at the above place, and by the time that I got up, he was holding an ear of corn over a sickly fire, roasting it for his supper, and most of the men did not even have that much. Several of the boys and myself went into a field, and brought out a lot of pumpkins, which we held up over the fire, in slices, of which we poor, half famished boys made a meal, and I acknowledge, we relished it.

Here we lay until Sunday, the 29th, when we commenced crossing the river in a very fantastic manner. We took off our Zouaves, put them on our heads, and into the river we jumped. The water was so cold that several of the boys took the cramp before they got across.

About noon we started of[f] for Camp Enyart, in better spirits than could be expected. We marched all day without anything to eat and about five o'clock we came to Platoona, but here as elsewhere, we could not get anything to eat. We went to bed without supper, or rather lay down on the hard ground, and slept till morning, without being disturbed by the "secesh."

On Monday, we left Platoona, expecting to make Camp by six o'clock in the evening, but in this we were disappointed, for the recent flood had torn up the roads in some places in such a manner as to make them almost impassable for our teams. When within about six miles of our Camp, we met a wagon load of provisions which had been sent out for our relief. When the boys found out that the provisions were for them, they gave one of the heartiest "Zouaves" that hungry mortals ever gave before. The next day we made Camp Enyart, to find it had been overflowed by the great Kanawa [sic], which had been forty feet above the low water mark. Our tents were in the mud, which made the Camp a place which was not very inviting to boys who had been wading in the mud and water over thirty hours.[284]

In addition to having won the battle, the Federals captured four horses, one wagon, ten rifles, twelve muskets and the commissary stores of the Confederate camp. Thus ended this extraordinary battle in the mountains, the culmination of the Coal River Valley "campaign" of 1861 and one of the more interesting and impactful series of operations of the war in West Virginia. Small, fierce and short, the Battle of Kanawha Gap was decisive in its local effects. "The country between Charleston and the Guyandotte River is now freed from secession power," the *New York Times* reported. "This is the most effective blow given the rebels in this part of the Valley."[285]

Not to be outdone in praise for the signal victory, the *National Republican* in Washington, D.C., predicted that the battle's results "will, it is supposed, restore permanent peace to the Virginia counties west of the Kanawha."[286] While it did not result in permanent peace of course—far from it, in fact—the battle's results did negate any advantages the Confederates had gained at Coal River and Pond Fork and affirmed the lasting outcome of the fight at Boone Court House. The war's frontline in southwestern Virginia had been moved to the Guyandotte line. Floyd's master plan to winter in the Boone-Logan region was wrecked. The Union army's action compelled the Confederates to fall back to Logan Court House as their principal forward hold in the region for the remainder of the war.

Chapter 6

AFTERMATH

The losses suffered by the armies of the North and South, and their local Home Guard militia allies, in the Coal River Valley region between August and September 1861 were not light, for they numbered together nearly 200 officers and men, of whom at least 16 were killed, 35 wounded and 134 captured, paroled or missing. The Federals lost the bulk of two companies, of the First Kentucky and Eighth (West) Virginia Regiments, which were captured. Also captured were Captains Thomas Cox Jr., of the First Kentucky, and Peter Miller of the Eighth (West) Virginia. They were taken to Richmond's dreadful Libby Prison and exchanged later in the war.

What the total Federal and Confederate casualties were respectively is unknown exactly, but for the entire series of actions, the total Federal casualties amounted to about 102, or about 6 percent of the 1,600 Union troops engaged. The total Confederate casualties included about 83 killed, wounded and captured or missing, about 18 percent of the estimated 465 Rebel troops engaged. In addition, an estimated 95 civilians and slaves were taken by either side as political prisoners and contraband. In all, therefore, military and civilian casualties totaled at least 280—a remarkable quantity for these events to have been so completely overlooked by history since the war.[287]

The campaign made these things clear. The Union determination to subdue the Coal River Valley's secessionist fever and the magnitude of the Confederate rout created a strong public impression of the North's resolve to consolidate its hold on western Virginia. The effects helped sustain the North's public support for the formation of the new state of West Virginia.

The actions in the Coal River Valley had involved Ohio, Kentucky and Virginia (and western Virginia) regiments and local Union and secessionist militia. In no measure had the operations been large enough to merit comparison to a Bull Run or later larger battles. In contrast, the actions were overshadowed in history by the other battles in western Virginia at about the same time at Carnifex Ferry (September 10), Cheat Mountain (September 10–15) and Romney (September 24).

Some notice came to personalities in the drama. General Cox was recognized for his great promise as a Union commander and for his organizing and administrative skills in generally overseeing the events, ancillary to the larger struggle for Gauley Bridge that commanded his fuller attention, while Guthrie was noted for a pompous proclamation he published afterward—that the threat of a Rebel invasion of Ohio had been stopped.[288] The retaliatory burning of Boone Court House made Enyart's name loathsome to the South. For the audacious charge he ordered at Boone Court House, the "gallant" and "brilliant" Captain Wheeler of the First Kentucky became one of the war's early Union heroes. "Rook's Charge" earned the Twenty-sixth Ohio's Captain Rook similar distinction. Intrepid Union scout William Workman would become a long-serving West Virginia state legislator. On the Confederate side, the daring and resourceful cavalry commanders Pate, Caskie and Tucker won prestige, and all rose to command their own regiments in the war. Colonel James Ward Davis was so severely wounded that he never sufficiently recovered to return to service.

While the Coal River Valley operations were a small affair compared to later events in the war, it was militarily important to the war in southwestern Virginia. The outcome pushed the war's "front line" in the mountains back over one thousand square miles in an arc from Brownstown, forty miles to Logan Court House, sixty miles to Wyoming Court House and sixty miles to Raleigh Court House. However, it failed to completely reduce the Coal River Valley as an avenue for the Confederates to threaten the Kanawha Valley as the Federals hoped. "The whole population between Little Coal and Guyandotte are in the highest degree hostile to the Union; that especially at Big Creek, Mill Creek, Upper Hewitt, and on both sides of the Guyandotte," reported Colonel Edward Siber, Thirty-seventh Ohio Infantry Regiment.[289]

Boone County, in particular, became a grim no-man's land, fought over but left unoccupied by either side throughout the war except for outposts. The Union army in western Virginia did not have enough strength to permanently garrison and control the one thousand square miles of the disputed Coal River Valley and bordering areas or to protect their Unionist militia allies. The Confederates were more incapable. For the civilians caught in the maelstrom of the war, this condition plunged the region into a state of prolonged terror that would not end until after the war's conclusion. It became, as Mark Snell, the most recent historian of the war in West Virginia, observed, "a fierce battleground, with ongoing guerrilla warfare just as intense and brutal as that practiced in Missouri and east Tennessee."[290]

Throughout the war, as the narrator in *The Last Grace*, a historical novel about the war in the Pond Fork River Valley, explained:

> [Boone Court House] *got a visit every few weeks by a small detachment of Southern boys and larger units of one or two companies of Union soldiers. When the government in Richmond took most of the regiments out of the mountains to fight in the Shenandoah Valley and east of the Blue Ridge Mountains, it fell to small Confederate militia detachments and sometimes companies moving around to keep the people safe from the Yankees. Most of the detachments had old, musket firearms and more mules than horses to carry the soldiers who were lucky enough not to have to walk.*[291]

In 1861–62, the Union commander in western Virginia, General Rosecrans, knew the area intimately and regarded the Confederate ability to base at Logan Court House and strike through Boone County as more dangerous to the Federals in the Kanawha Valley than anything else. Before the war, Rosecrans had served as president of the Coal River Navigation Company. He foresaw that the road from Brownstown to Boone and Logan would have to be constantly guarded.[292] As a

Union major general William S. Rosecrans, commander, 1861–62, (West) Virginia, regarded the Confederate ability to strike the Federal rear through the Coal River Valley as more dangerous than anything else. *Library of Congress.*

consequence, the Coal River Valley emerged as one of western Virginia's most unrestrained, violent areas of constant guerrilla activity, requiring the Federal army's unceasing attention and energies. The crossroads towns of Peytona, Coon's Mill, Pond Fork and Boone Court House especially saw lots of military activity during the war.

The rosters of regiments and other units of renown in the war included recruits from throughout the Coal River Valley region:

Union

4th Regiment, West Virginia Infantry, Company K

6th Regiment, West Virginia Infantry, Company B

8th Regiment, West Virginia Infantry (later the Seventh West Virginia Cavalry), Companies B, E, G, I and H

11th Regiment, West Virginia Infantry, Companies F and G

13th Regiment, West Virginia Infantry, Company H

45th Regiment, Kentucky Mounted Infantry, Company H

1st Regiment, West Virginia Cavalry, Company A

2nd Regiment, West Virginia Cavalry, Companies D and I

3rd Regiment, West Virginia Cavalry, Company B

4th Regiment, West Virginia Cavalry, Companies C and K

187th Mounted Infantry Battalion, West Virginia State Troops, Peytona Home Guards (companies of Adkins, Barker, Harless, Jonathan Spurlock, Robertson Spurlock, Toney, Williams and Buchanan)

190th Regiment, West Virginia State Troops, Raleigh, Wyoming and McDowell County Scouts

Confederate

1st Regiment, Virginia State Line (Cavalry), Company B

2nd Regiment, Virginia State Line (Cavalry), Company K

22nd Regiment, Virginia Infantry (First Kanawha Regiment), Company K (Boone Company)

36th Regiment, Virginia Infantry (Second Kanawha Regiment), Company K (Boone Company)

30th Battalion, Virginia Sharpshooters, Company A

8th Regiment, Virginia Cavalry, Company G

14th Regiment, Virginia Cavalry, Company F

36th Battalion, Virginia Cavalry, Company E

Swann's Battalion, Virginia Cavalry, Watkins' Company
34th Battalion, Virginia Cavalry (Witcher's Battalion, Virginia Mounted
    Rifles), Company B
45th Battalion, Virginia Infantry, Company A
Kanawha Artillery Battery, Hale's Company
187th Regiment (Boone), Virginia Militia
129th Regiment (Logan), Virginia Militia
190th Regiment (Wyoming), Virginia Militia

In the mountains, mobility and subsistence were difficult, so the basic unit was the company, commanded by a captain (one hundred men = two platoons = four sections = eight squads). A company had the following officers (commissioned and noncommissioned): captain (one), first lieutenant (one), second lieutenant (one), first sergeant (one), sergeants (four) and corporals (eight). When the company divided into platoons, the captain commanded one and the first lieutenant the other. There was a sergeant for each section and a corporal for each squad. The first sergeant administered the whole company. Units were rarely, if ever, at full strength.

The primary tactical and maneuvering units in the mountains became the regiment and battalion. Most regiments naturally consisted of two subdivisions—battalions numbering five hundred men each. In the field, a battalion typically consisted of four to eight companies. Throughout the Coal River Valley operations, such small, manageable formations predominated as both sides favored units that were light, mobile and flexible. Thereafter in the mountainous southern West Virginia area of operations, battalion-sized Union forces were mostly the standard for operating rapidly and nimbly as striking forces against enemy communication and supply lines.

Southern and Union sympathizers alike also formed small, irregular guerrilla organizations first to defend their families and communities and then to support the war effort against the other's forces. Thus, the Coal River Valley became an unrelenting cauldron of the Civil War in microcosm—truly marked by brother against brother and a vicious neighbor-against-neighbor character. Some of these units were pro-Confederate or pro-Union in name only and preyed on civilians of both sides, as small, localized bands marauded the region during the war. The forces on both sides employed classic guerrilla hit-and-run attacks, raids and ambushes. Innumerable skirmishes resulted during the war at places with homespun-sounding names like Turtle Creek, Crooked Creek, Laurel Creek, Buffalo Creek, Thompson's Ford, Sand Lick, Sugartree Creek, Rock Lick, Elk Run and Six-Mile.

The pro-Confederate elements demonstrated their strength in the October 1861 election to ratify the proposed secession of western Virginia from the Old Dominion and the creation of a new state (named West Virginia in 1863). Of eight polling places in Boone County designated to hold the statehood election, only two precincts—Peytona, defended by a Federal detachment sent from the Kanawha Valley, and Mud River, defended by Home Guards—were able to administer voting. In defending the pro-Union voters from election violence, the detachment of Federal troops in Boone County lost one killed and several captured.[293]

Meanwhile, in Raleigh County, "the only balloting was among the Northern loyalists along the Clear Fork of Coal," as Clarkson's Confederate cavalry terrorized the voting.[294] First Lieutenant William S. Dunbar, commander, Company H, Eighth (West) Virginia Infantry, wrote in his diary:

The precinct was three miles below where my family lived [at Clear Fork of Coal], *so I went on and we had the election, but just as we closed the polls a man came running across a field and told me there were five hundred rebel cavalry following us and by that time were not more than a mile from us. The man who gave me the news was Jubal Stover of Cabin Creek, Kanawha County. He had run seven or eight miles across a long mountain and was nearly exhausted by fatigue...*

I ordered the men into line and we went to the edge of the wood by the road, expecting to have a fight. We waited there about two or three hours for them but they did not come, so we gave them up and left up the river (Clear Fork of Coal) in the direction of where my family lived. I knew we would have to be very cautious or we would all be killed or taken prisoners. Consequently, I told my men to scatter, with only two or three together, and not stay at any one person's house, but to meet me on the other side of the mountain two days later and we would go back to our camps, which we could have done with safety...Then I went home to see what had become of my family. I found them all well, but very uneasy. It was by this time nearly dark. My wife said she would hurry and get me a bite to eat so I could leave the house and not be seen there. I told her to give me some bed clothes and I would go to the woods and make me a bed to lie in while she got my supper, and she did so.

I fixed a place to sleep and then went back to the house. Supper was ready and I ate it, then sat down by the fire to change my shoes and socks because the ones I had on were wet.

Just as I got my shoes on and tied, the rebels came into the house. I was at the fire and said good evening to them. They said the same to me. It was dark in the house, no lights, so I could not tell who they were.

One of them asked me if they could get a bite to eat. I told them if it was cooked that they could. My wife and daughter, being frightened very bad, said that there was nothing cooked but that they could cook it in a few minutes.

I asked them who they were and they, in order to get advantage of me, told me a lie and tried to make me believe they were Union soldiers. I could see plain enough to tell that they had on Union soldiers' uniforms. They told me they were scout cavalry, and asked me who lived there, trying by that means to fool me, because they knew me and knew where I lived as well as I did myself nearly. But I answered and told them a man by the name of Dunbar lived there. I knew their business very well and was trying to fool them, which I did, you will see.

They asked me if I could make them a light, and then I knew there was no more time to be spent there because the yard by this time was full of horses and men who I could hear rushing up to the door and around the house. So I turned around as though I was making a light and creeped out the back door and ran out into the corn field. I got away from them and left them in the house, amazed and badly fooled. I stood within about 60 yards of the house and heard them all pass by. The men who came into the house left as soon as they found that I was gone.

As soon as all was quiet my wife came to the edge of the woods and made a noise. I went to her and asked what they said after I left. She told me that they did not ask where I was or what had become of me or anything about me but told her that they had no time to waste for supper and that they would have to go on because they expected to go to Raleigh Court House that night and get a distance of 20 miles to surprise the rebels and drive them off. They thought that by telling her that I would believe they were Federal soldiers, but I knew they were rebels and would come after me that night.

I told my wife they were trying to lay a trap to catch me and that they would go off a few miles and come back again before daylight. I said that I would go to my bed in the woods and if they came back I would hear them. We parted and she went to the house and I went to the woods and laid down and slept tolerably well.

Just before daylight I heard them coming. I listened and watched for them. The moon gave a little light so I could see glimpses of them as they jarred by the house, which they surrounded the first thing. My daughter, about 15 years old (Susan Alice Dunbar, 14), heard them and went to the door and one of the rascals shot at her, coming very near killing her. The bullet hit a log just at the side of the door after passing her, and then they all rushed up to the house. (Susan Alice Dunbar, according to family accounts, was shot at several times by the Confederates while carrying messages from her father to the Union Army. After the war she and her father were invited to a party at the White House. Susan had made a yellow gown to wear but then faked illness because she didn't want to go. However, her father did attend the party...) Some of them came into the house and searched for me in the kitchen an under the house and up the stairs and all around, everywhere they thought a man could hide, but they did not find me.

Then they abused my wife and daughter, telling them that I was a traitor and a damned abolitionist and threatened to burn the house with them in it.

After looking into everything in the house, they stole all the money my wife had and all their clothing, all the bed clothing, and everything that they could carry off on horses. They left, and my wife came out and told me all that had happened, although I could see them all the time. They were there running around the house and stable. It was nearly sunrise when they left.

I told my wife I would stay in the woods not far from the house that day and the next morning, but if they came back anymore that day or night to come out to the field, about a quarter of a mile from the house, and let me know what they had done. The next morning I heard her calling and I knew they had been hunting for me again, so I did not stay very near the house that day. In the evening, she came and told me they had been after me again and had brought some of the nearest neighbors with them to help hunt me, offering them five hundred dollars if they could find me or kill me. So when they commenced hunting the woods for me, I went off to the place where I was to meet my company, and found a part of them there. We then went back to our camps at Charleston, and in a few days the balance of my men came into camp.[295]

However, not all the members of Dunbar's company of Union volunteers were as fortunate. Clarkson's cavalrymen pursued and attacked a small detachment at Spruce Mountain:

They told me they had a dangerous time, and that after we parted on Coal River they went up the river...about two miles and stopped at John Stover's [on John's Creek, on the Clear Fork of Coal] *to get breakfast. The rebel cavalry rode up to surround the house. One of my men by the name of Creed Maynor ran out of the house and tried to make his escape but the rebels shot him before he got out of the yard. He lived a few days and then died…The rest of the men of my company who were in the house were taken prisoners, except Charles Stover. He ran upstairs into the kitchen and remained there until the rebels went into the house. Stover crept out at the gravel end of the house through a small hole in the weather boarding, then jumped down and crept under the floor of the porch, staying there until the rebels sat down to eat. Then he crept out and ran into the woods, making a safe escape, but the rest of the men were taken off…They also took several citizens at the same time.[296]*

After the Battle of Kanawha Gap, the 187th (Boone) Militia Regiment companies remained "under arms, operating in Boone and Logan Counties," posing constant threats to attack the Federal militia at Peytona and harassing Union settlements on the Pond and Spruce Forks of Little Coal. The Rebel militia finally disbanded on November 2 at Camp Newport, now Danville.[297] Nearly all the Federal expeditions in the Coal River Valley that followed the extensive operations in the summer and autumn of 1861 were in response to marauding, reports of Confederate activity or to support Union Home Guard operations.

As the rule of law broke down and state and local government and administration collapsed throughout the Coal River Valley, the rival forces in the region attacked each other vengefully, destroying or seizing farms, homes and crops; burning and robbing; and carrying out fiendish offenses against the civilian population.[298] In many instances, the war devolved, more or less, into a means of resolving personal disputes and courthouse politics under the cloak of war. The murders of neighbors over minor disagreements, robbery and the burning of homesteads caused great bitterness between communities and clans.

It was more dangerous to life, liberty and property to live in the section referred to than to have been in the army of one or the other of the belligerents. A peaceable non-combatant was liable at any hour night or day to be arrested, carried away and incarcerated in prison without any charges preferred against him, and worse than all, he was frequently allowed to lie in prison and perish without knowing with what offense he was charged, if any. In partial illustration of this statement it is stated that one Augustus Pack, of Boone County, an old man and a non-combatant, who carried on trade between the lines, was frequently arrested, first by one side and then by the other, and carried to military prison where he remained some times for months, and then released upon taking the oath of allegiance to the Government that had him a prisoner. General Cox, the Federal commandant in the Kanawha Valley, had had Mr. Pack so frequently before him that he had become very well acquainted with him, and so, as the story goes, on an occasion after Mr. Pack had been arrested by the Federal troops and was being carried to General Cox's headquarters, he was discovered by General Cox approaching his tent under guard, whereupon the General exclaimed, "Here you are again, Pack," to which he replied, "Well, General, I am an old man and have nothing to do with the war, and try to remain at home a quiet, peaceable citizen, when along comes the Rebels who arrest and carry me within their lines and require me to take the oath of allegiance, and as soon as I return home I am picked up by your men and brought within your lines, and required to take the oath of allegiance, and this process has been going on for several months; the truth is, General, that the foxes have holes and the birds of the air have nests, but as for me I have nowhere to lay my head."[299]

The guerrilla operations required the Federals to conduct frequent reconnaissance patrols, raids and sweeps throughout the area to track and defeat the irregular forces and suppress their support for the Confederate war effort. Consequently, in the course of the war, the Coal River Valley was trampled under hoof and foot, its population terrorized by the movements, actions and depredations of both sides. In the end, the years of raiding and bushwhacking devastated the area, leaving Boone County especially "in as primitive a state as it ever was" for the next fifty years.[300] In 1870, five years after the war's end and Boone's partial dismemberment in 1867 to form Lincoln County, the county population was 6 percent smaller than it had been in 1860.[301]

In January 1862, General Cox sent the Thirty-seventh Ohio Infantry Regiment, commanded by Colonel Edward Siber, into the region in order to quell marauding. The Federal objective was to disperse one band of irregulars in particular, the Black Striped Company of the 129th Virginia Militia Regiment, operating in the country between the Guyandotte, Mud and Coal Rivers. The Federals crossed the Little Coal River at Boone Court House on January 12. Four companies headed for Chapmanville, one company advanced along Turtle Creek to the head of Mud River and another company with Siber camped at Ballard's Farm on the Spruce Fork of the Little Coal River near Boone Court House.

The next day at Chapmanville, the leading Federal detachments were fired on from houses and hills while advancing up the right bank of the Guyandotte River against Logan Court House, suffering a loss of one man killed. Some of the Federals swam across the river and attacked and burned the houses from which the hostile fire came, capturing several prisoners. Siber marched on the town, advancing up both sides of the Guyandotte River. The Federals found the town evacuated by the male population and militia dug in on the mountainside opposite the community. A sharp skirmish was fought in which another Federal was killed. Before withdrawing on January 15, the Federals burned the Logan County Courthouse and neighboring buildings. The Federals retired along Crooked Creek into Boone County and then followed Hewett Creek and Spruce Fork to Boone Court House, where they crossed the Little Coal River. The regiment was delayed at Peytona for several days by high water on the Big Coal River but reached Charleston on January 23.[302]

Confederate raider Captain Andrew Gunnoe, in particular, earned infamy during the Civil War for guerrilla warfare, murdering Union soldiers and his atrocities against citizens in southern West Virginia. Although he served the Confederacy, Gunnoe seemingly fought for personal revenge and plunder as much as commitment to the South. At the outbreak of the Civil War, he organized a group of Confederate irregulars in Wyoming County. An excellent shot and horseman, he became the gang's leader. Later with Company C of the Forty-fifth Virginia Infantry Battalion, Gunnoe and his band undertook guerrilla raids that made his name notably feared throughout the Coal River Valley region.

> *Gunnoe, a southern sympathizer, did not join in the fight as a soldier during the Civil War. He may have been too old (42 years old at the beginning of the Civil War) to serve. Andrew, the leader of the ruthless Confederate Home Guard, and his sons, terrorized the families of men that had joined the Union Army in Summers, Mercer, Wyoming, Raleigh and Boone Counties. Roaming this area, they stole pigs, cows, and horses at their leisure. Andrew and his men would also shanghai men and turn them over to the Confederate Army for compulsory service. Union soldiers home on leave were subjected to being shot from ambush (bushwhacking), captured and turned over to the Confederate Army as prisoners of war, or captured and shot while trying to "escape." He and his men would also enter the homes of Union sympathizers and steal clothes and household articles.[303]*

Gunnoe figured prominently in one of the war's more severe incidents in the region. Occurring in the summer of 1863 in the Walnut Gap along the Boone-Wyoming Counties line, the incident was typical of the war's merciless ferocity in the region:

> *John Lester and Edley Whitt, with their wives and children, were traveling from the upper end of Wyoming (Co, WV) to some point in Kanawha County. On the road near the mouth of Toney fork, they met Capt. Andrew Gunnoe and a squad of his Home Guards, who, knowing the men were Union sympathizers, took them prisoner and rode away with them leaving their terrified women and children in the road to care for themselves.*
>
> *At a point just below the Sanders farm, Captain Gunnoe, Charles S. Canterbury, and Adoniram J. Lusk continued on the road toward Elk Lick on horseback, the foot soldiers taking the prisoners over a path across the hill, a shorter way to Elk Lick. At the top of the hill the guards shot the prisoners and left them for dead, then continued their way to join the officers at Meeting House Branch where they ate dinner.*
>
> *Soon after the shooting, passersby found the prisoners. Lester was dead. Whitt, mortally wounded, was still living and had crawled to water. Lester was buried near the scene.*
>
> *Whitt was taken to Oceana where he was placed on a makeshift bed in the clerk's small brick office with the permission of James Cook, clerk. Here he lingered and suffered twenty days before death relieved him. During this time, his wife was permitted to be with him and helped take care of him. A religious woman, she not only cared for him physically but comforted him by singing hymns and reading or quoting passages from the Bible. Other people were permitted to visit and talk with him, and he made statements about the shooting as he lay on his death bed. One of his visitors was Mattie, the wife of James Cook, the clerk. His statements were not reduced to writing, but in 1865, when James Gunnoe was tried for his part in the affair, Whitt's statements were accepted as dying testimony with the result that Gunnoe was convicted. He was one of the men detailed to guard the prisoners.[304]*

Both Lester and Whitt were members of the younger Walker's company of the 190th (Wyoming) Militia Regiment. It is suspected that Whitt had been among the Union troops present at the fight at Boone Court House and who, with fellow ardent Union sympathizer Private Micajah White, of Bald Knob and Barker's company, 187th (Boone) Militia Regiment, might have actually set fire to the courthouse.[305] One side's villain, the other side's patriot, Gunnoe's reputation was especially made with such heinous actions as the murder of Lester and Whitt during his frequent forays. In 1864, after Gunnoe and his men raided the inhabitants of the upper Big Coal River country, a band of Union soldiers from the Marsh Fork region on leave ambushed and killed him while he was on furlough at his home on Craney Creek:

Upon hearing of Andrew Gunnoe's terrorist acts from their families, the Union men asked for leave to return and kill him. Their Commanding Officer was told that they were going home to kill Gunnoe with or without his permission, but they would return to his command if they were granted leave. This was in August 1864.

The men were from the 7th West Virginia Cavalry led by Lt. Jacob Webb. With Lt. Webb were Pvt. Ballard Preston Petry, Pvt. Milan, and Pvt. Pennington. Lt. Webb, and Pvts. Petry and Pennington had brothers serving in the Confederate Army. While home, they were very visible, attending church and visiting friends for about four days. During this time, Andrew Gunnoe went into hiding. On an appointed day, they met as a group and marched away as if returning to their command in the Shenandoah Valley near Waynesboro, Virginia. They went as far as Clover Bottom on the Bluestone River before stopping to wait for dark. After dark, they returned and stationed themselves in the woods around Andrew's cabin. Andrew lived on Craney Creek in Wyoming County. Joining them here were Pemberton Cook and his son Perry, who had been enlisted to help.

As the sun came up, Gunnoe's son, John, came out of the back door of the cabin and gathered an arm full of stove wood before returning inside. Smoke from the chimney gave evidence that breakfast was cooking. Sometime later, Gunnoe's dogs began to bark sounding the alarm alerting him of the presence of men stationed in the woods behind the cabin. Gunnoe and John bolted out the front door and ran down a path to the forest. Gunnoe had on a coat with a single large white button, fashioned from a clamshell, holding the coat together in the center of his chest. He was carrying a rifle in one hand and a piece of cake in the other.

Lt. Webb, Pemberton and Perry Cook had stationed themselves at the back of the cabin. They thought Gunnoe would try to escape into the woods from the back entrance of the cabin.

Petry and Pennington had stationed themselves in the woods at the path gate at the front of the cabin. They agreed to take aim at the button and fire as Gunnoe drew near. When he was within a few yards of them, they fired, the button disappeared, and Gunnoe fell dead. John's life was spared only because Lt. Webb rushed to the scene and called out, "Spare the boy!" The Reverend James Peters (Andrew Gunnoe had shot Rev. Peters' nephew) later reported that the bullets had made a single hole large enough to drop a pebble through.[306]

Similarly, Union first lieutenant Ferdinand Newman (Neumann) earned infamy among Southerners. He and other Peytona Home Guards, later Companies B and I, Eighth West Virginia Infantry Regiment, ranged throughout the Coal River Valley in 1861–62 terrorizing the population. Newman's band specialized in burning the property of Confederate soldiers and sympathizers. He was active throughout southwestern Virginia but especially in the Big Coal country, upper Pond Fork, Wyoming County and Tazewell areas. Newman's reputation was sealed during one of his forays into Wyoming County. In early 1862, Newman led Union partisans in pillaging and burning the McDonald plantation, home of Wyoming County's most Confederate and affluent family. Newman gave them a few minutes to gather personal belongings and then burned the house. A few months later, while returning from a raid at Tazewell, Virginia, Newman was ambushed and killed by a Confederate bushwhacker along Indian Creek.[307]

In August 1862, Union scouting parties operated south and east through this territory. One of the detachments, forty-eight men from the Fourth (West) Virginia Infantry under Major John T. Hall, was attacked by a large number of Confederate cavalry. The Rebels included Stratton and Witcher's companies and Beckley and Chambers "gangs of bushwhackers" (the "Logan Wildcats"). After probing up the Spruce Fork from Boone Court House, the Federals were ambushed in Logan County at Kenneth's Hill (Kenneday's). In the Battle of Beech Creek, the Federals were routed with a loss of three killed and eight wounded, among them Hall, who died after being pierced by four balls. The major was the son of John Hall, president of the first state constitutional convention and framer of the first state constitution of West Virginia. The Rebels lost one killed and eleven wounded.[308]

In September 1862, while Confederate general William W. Loring was driving the Federal army down the Kanawha Valley in support of Lee's Antietam campaign, Jenkins' Raiders, 1,200 to 1,500 strong, thundered through Raleigh and Boone Counties along the Coal River Road to cut off Union brigadier general Andrew J. Lightburn's retreat from the Kanawha Valley. At Mouth of Short Creek, a column of Jenkins' men headed for Brownstown, where he discovered that the lead Federal columns had fled the valley so rapidly it would not be possible to block their escape. Meanwhile, another column of Jenkins' Raiders followed the Coal River to

Confederate brigadier general Albert G. Jenkins,
commander, Jenkins' Cavalry Brigade, maneuvered his
command through the Coal River Valley in the autumn
of 1862 to strike the rear of Lightburn's Retreat from the
Kanawha Valley. *Library of Congress*.

Coalsmouth and struck the Federal rear, panicking the retreat, which resulted in the Union army's loss of a large amount of military stores and supplies.[309]

In the summer of 1862, the Virginia state legislature had authorized a partisan force commanded by General John B. Floyd to recapture western Virginia from Union control. Called the Virginia State Line, Floyd's two thousand troops waged irregular warfare in McDowell, Wyoming, Logan, Boone, Cabell and Wayne Counties. In autumn, Floyd advanced with his command into Boone County. After driving out the local Union Home Guards who fled the area, Floyd's force for a time occupied Boone Court House and vigorously foraged and recruited for Confederate service.[310] They remained until all food in the area was gone. The saying "enough to feed Floyd" to describe a large amount of food remains a common expression in the region, although few today know its Civil War origins.

In response to Floyd's activity in the area, the Federals in mid-November 1862 sent Lieutenant Colonel Augustus C. Parry, Forty-seventh Ohio Infantry Regiment, with thirty-five infantry and one hundred cavalry to scout the Confederates reported to be assembling in force under Floyd at Boone Court House and to bring to justice the parties who had robbed and shot a Union man near Peytona. Joined by forty-five men at Mouth of Short Creek, the Federal force camped for the night at Laurel Creek. Advancing down Pond Fork, they arrived at Boone Court House the next day at noon. The Confederate force had already departed the area, but the Federals captured two stragglers after a brief exchange of shooting.

Parry pushed his cavalry forward to intercept a Rebel force reported advancing from Chapmanville. Meanwhile, reinforced with 120 more cavalry, Parry sent these to learn if Confederate generals Floyd and Humphrey Marshall were combining their forces near Logan Court House. Parry withdrew the Union infantry eight miles toward Peytona. Receiving orders to return to Brownstown, early on the seventeenth, he sent out couriers to the infantry and cavalry with orders to return to Brownstown. In the course of the scouting in Boone County, the Forty-seventh Ohio Regiment took eight prisoners. They reached Gauley Mountain on the twentieth.[311]

Later that same month, a larger Federal force took the Boone–Logan road to Boone Court House again in search of Floyd's force, reported operating sixty miles to the southwest. From there, a brigade of the Twenty-eighth and Thirtieth Ohio Infantry Regiments and Schambeck's Independent Illinois Cavalry Company moved by separate routes against Logan Court House—the Twenty-eighth taking the lower route via Boone Court House and Low Gap and the Thirtieth moving through Chapmanville. The plan was to rejoin at Huff's Creek, a branch of the Guyandotte River located near present-day Man and about fifteen miles from Logan Court House. The Federals reached Logan Court House on December 4 and for a few days skirmished throughout the area with elements of Clarkson's Confederate cavalry, stragglers and soldiers on furlough. In these expeditions along the region's innumerable creeks and hollows, a few Rebels were killed, some prisoners captured and mills burned.[312] First Lieutenant Henry R. Brinkerhoff described the activities of the Thirtieth Ohio, ordered to advance from Brownstown through the Coal River Valley in search of Floyd:

On the thirtieth of November, an order was received from General Scammon (General Ewing being absent) to proceed at once to Brownstown with all our available force, and in conjunction with the 28th Ohio, march into

Logan county, observing such directions as General Crooks might give at Brownstown. Major Hildt was absent at Gauley bridge, on a general court-martial, and the regiment was under command of Captain Cunningham. Preparations were at once made, and the regiment moved as far as Clifton, five miles distant, and quartered for the night in empty houses. During the evening, Major Hildt joined the regiment and took command. On the following evening, we reached Browns town and bivouacked near the mouth of Len's Creek. On the first of December, we left the river and moved up this creek until we reached the summit of the river hills, having crossed the stream fifty-two times in three miles. We then moved down Short Creek until we reached Coal River, where we separated from the 28th [Ohio Regiment], *which had accompanied us thus far, with the understanding that they were to approach Logan Court House from one direction, while we came in from another. That night we slept in the deserted houses of the operatives of the Petonia Cannel Coal Company, on Little Coal River. We were surprised to find here several fine brick dwellings with families living in them, who were able to appreciate the comforts of life. Throughout the entire march, we moved up and down the creeks, crossing them repeatedly; along the ravine of one until we reached the summit of Droity Mountain, and then down another, until we reached its base; so we crossed Price Mountain and several very high hills.*

On the fourth day we reached Red House on Little Coal River. On the fifth, Chapmansville on Guyandotte River, and on the sixth, entered Logan. We expected to find a company of Floyd's men here [Confederate Cavalry troops operating in the region], *but the majority had escaped some hours before. Two rebel cavalrymen, however, were captured on our approaching the town, and two infantrymen endeavored to escape by flight. One was killed and the other captured.*

During the night, dispatches were received from the 28th [Ohio], *to the effect that they were encamped twenty miles above, and would reach the town the following evening. The next morning we burned Floyd's steam grist mill and one dwelling, and shortly after started to return. Major Hildt left a small detachment of men under charge of Serg't Price, at the Court House, with instructions to remain in or near the town, and to follow on to Chapmansville after the 28th arrived at Logan. Shortly after the regiment moved out, this detachment was fired into by guerrillas, but no one injured, and the Sergeant retreated some five miles towards Chapmansville. After the 28th reached Logan, he returned and related the facts to the officer in command.*

During the latter part of the day and all of the following night, snow fell until on the morning of the sixth of December it lay full four inches deep upon the ground. A company of the 28th [Ohio] was now detailed to pursue the guerrillas. They eventually succeeded in striking their trail and following them to their rendezvous. Here they captured and destroyed considerable provisions and some arms; several prisoners were also taken and one or two rebels killed.

The snow and rain upon the mountains had frozen as it fell, and the roads were now almost impassable. Large details were made, and the ice, in many instances, dug from the road before an ascent could be effected. The poor horses and mules, weary, distrustful and with bleeding knees from frequent falling, reached the summit of the hills, after repeated exertions. The descent was more hazardous than the ascent. Rough locks were fastened upon the wheels, and ropes tied to the axles and carried to the rear, and a dozen stout men guided and held the wagon back from running forward on the horses. With these precautions, one wagon after another safely reached the bottom, save in one instance, when the staff wagon got the better of its guardians and tumbled over a bank full twenty feet, dragging with it driver, horses and all, but fortunately, without any damage to either. Many of the men wore out their shoes in the march, and when we again reached our camp at Cannelton, some of them had actually marched several miles in their bare feet. During the march, several side expeditions were sent out with good results. We turned over seventeen prisoners at Brownstown, among whom was a Colonel and two non-commissioned officers, and returned to camp on the ninth of December with seventy-five horses.[313]

In February 1863, the Second (West) Virginia Cavalry Regiment mounted a five-day scouting expedition by seventy Federals under Major John McMahan from Camp Piatt through Boone and Wyoming Counties as far as Wyoming Court House and back. In blinding snowstorms, they found no secessionist forces but captured three horses. The men were out three days (February 5–8) and nearly froze to death. Confederate general Floyd, commanding Virginia militia in southern West Virginia, withdrew his forces when the Federal scouting party penetrated the area.

In March, McMahan left Brownstown on another scout with 140 men of the Second (West) Virginia Cavalry Regiment and Home Guards on the night of the twelfth, crossed Kanawha River, crossed Big Coal River at Thompson's farm and went as far as Boone Court House, sixteen miles, and camped. On the thirteenth, the Federals traveled thirty miles up the Pond

Fork. On the fourteenth, they marched to Wyoming Court House (Oceana), a distance of seventeen miles, arriving there at midnight and meeting no Rebels. The Federals crossed over the mountains and down Huff's Creek to Guyandotte River, a distance of sixteen miles, before halting for the night. Major McMahan reported:

> *I sent Captain Davidson, of Company E, with 25 men, up Guyandotte River, to ascertain if the report was true that 13 rebels were encamped at the house of a Mr. Christian, 6 miles above.*
>
> *On the way up, he discovered 8 rebels (mounted) on the opposite side of the river; passed them without being noticed; founded the river and got in their rear, and succeeded in capturing 5 horses and equipments 1 lieutenant and 3 privates; 4 others took to the mountains, and escaped in the darkness. Their saddle-bags contained some 400 rounds of ammunition, which, with their guns, were turned over to the Home Guards who accompanied the expedition. One little negro, belonging to the lieutenant, was brought into camp. Quite a number of Floyd's old command, living in these counties, are making their way home, singly and in squads, all armed and equipped for bushwhacking, &c.*
>
> *On the 15th, marched up Buffalo Creek on the mountains on to Pond Creek; thence to camp on the 16th, with the loss of but one horse, abandoned from fatigue.*[314]

A Federal cavalry force of two companies under Captain David Dove, Second (West) Virginia Cavalry Regiment, scouted the region in pursuit of Jenkins in April 1863. At Chapmanville (April 4), by way of Boone County, the Federals contacted the Confederate raiders and the "Logan Wildcats," Company D, Thirty-sixth Virginia Infantry Regiment, along the Mud River, and a sharp skirmish resulted. A dozen Rebels were killed or captured, seven horses taken and rifles and equipment captured. In a related affair, the next day at Milton (April 5), a Confederate ranger company under Captain Peter Carpenter marched on this settlement on the James River and Kanawha Turnpike and attempted to seize and destroy the Mud River Bridge but was repulsed by one of the companies of the Second (West) Virginia Cavalry. The result of the expedition was one Rebel killed and thirty-four captured, thirty horses captured and seventy-five to one hundred stand of arms destroyed. No Federals were hurt.[315]

In June 1863, Union colonel William H. Powell led the Second (West) Virginia Cavalry Regiment from Camp Piatt on a scout of the Big and

Little Coal Rivers in response to news of a Confederate cavalry company operating in the region:

Sir: In obedience to your order of the 18th, I left Camp Piatt with the remaining portion of my command, numbering 103, including officers, at 2 p.m. of said date; crossed over to Big Coal River; up said river to Thompson's Ford, finding the balance of my command, including the two companies sent out on the 17th and the one on the morning of the 18th, which had been up to Pack's farm and returned to Thompson's Ford, having found no enemy at that point. I crossed Big Coal River; proceeded up Laurel Creek to Pond Fork of Little Coal River, on which creek the rebel cavalry had camped on the night of the 17th, having left Pack's farm on Big Coal River on the morning of the 17th. I reached a point within 1½ miles of where the rebel cavalry had camped, at 1 a.m. 19th, having marched my command from 9 p.m. of the 18th until 1 a.m. 19th, by candle-light (in consequence of the extreme darkness of the night), in order that I might attack the enemy at daylight.

I learned, however, at the point where I halted, that the enemy had disappeared from their camp on Pond Fork at 10 a.m. of the 18th, and had gone in the direction of Raleigh Court-House.

I scouted, however, 10 miles up Pond Fork this morning, 7½ miles beyond where they had been in camp. Could learn nothing definite of their whereabouts or direction. At 7 a.m., 19th, I started en route for camp; arrived at Thompson's Ford at 12 p.m., where I learned that 100 rebel cavalry had been at 4 a.m., who, upon hearing of my force being up on Pond Fork of Little Coal River, retreated in great haste up Big Coal River, in the direction of Wyoming Court-House.

I am inclined to the opinion, from all I could learn, that there is no other force between Wyoming Court-House and this point other than the force referred to in this report, and presume they are beyond that point ere this.

Rebel reports on Pond Fork say nine regiments between Newbern Station and Raleigh Court-House. An attack to be made on Fayette soon.[316]

The intense military activity continued throughout the region in the summer and fall of 1863. In early July, about the time of the fall of Vicksburg (July 4), Captain Carpenter again led a Confederate force through present-day Lincoln County (then Boone). He received information that Company G, Third West Virginia Cavalry, commanded by Major John S. Witcher, was coming that way. Upon reaching the headwaters of the Sand Lick, a branch of Sugartree Creek, the Confederates obstructed the road with trees and brush, and when the Federals approached, the Rebels opened upon them so vigorously that the latter were forced to retreat. Two Federals were killed and three others wounded, while the Confederates escaped with the loss of one man killed and another wounded. The Federals returned to the Kanawha Valley.[317]

Also in July 1863, in Toland's raid on the Virginia & Tennessee Railroad and Wytheville, Virginia,

> the [Confederate] brigade of [General John] *McCausland, stationed in Raleigh County, at the crossing of Piney River, was, by a force of the enemy, compelled to abandon its position, and retreat upon Princeton. This force which threatened McCausland was under the immediate command of the Federal Colonel Toland, who had with him the 2nd Virginia cavalry, the 34th regiment of Ohio volunteer infantry, and a detachment of the 1st Virginia cavalry; these troops had left the Kanawha and crossed onto Coal River, and thence to Raleigh Court House, and to the front and flank of McCausland's command which impelled his retreat.*
>
> *The Federals then returned to Coal River, and marched by way of Wyoming Court House into Tazewell County, capturing at the head of Abb's Valley, Captain Joel E. Stolling and his company, which were re-captured on the next day by a bold charge made by Colonel A.J. May, at the head of his Kentucky cavalry. The Federals marched rapidly upon Wytheville, then virtually unprotected, entering the same on the evening of the 18th, when a sharp, brisk fight occurred between the enemy and about 130 men badly armed, under Majors Boyer and Bosang, and Captain Oliver with the aid of a few of the citizens of the town. The enemy after the loss of Colonel Toland, who was killed, Colonel Powell dangerously wounded and left a prisoner, and having some 75 or 80 men killed, wounded and captured, retired from the town, first setting it on fire. The Confederates lost three killed, seven wounded, and about 75 captured, including some of the citizens of the town. The Confederates endeavored to intercept and capture this raiding party, by sending troops on and along its most probable routes of retreat. Colonel May, with a portion of his 5th Kentucky regiment, together with Captain Henry Bowen, commanding a company of Tazewell County men of the 8th Virginia cavalry, followed closely, having several collisions and smart skirmishing with its rear guard, but unable to force the party to halt and fight. They finally succeeded in eluding the Confederates, by taking unfrequented paths through Crabtree's gap, over East River Mountain by W.H. Witten's farm, Pealed Chestnuts*

Brigadier General Alfred N. Duffié led a Union cavalry brigade through the Coal River Valley against Rebel cavalry in 1863. *Library of Congress.*

and over the mountain which led them on to the Tug fork of Sandy, where they were virtually free from successful pursuit.[318]

In September 1863, detachments of the Second West Virginia Cavalry and Thirty-fourth Ohio (Mounted) Infantry Regiments conducted a scouting expedition in Boone County. Then, later in the autumn, Brigadier General Alfred N. Duffié led a Federal cavalry brigade on another scout from Charleston to Boone Court House in pursuit of three hundred to four hundred Confederate cavalry under Lieutenant Colonel Henry M. Beckley who were reported to be recruiting and stealing horses in the area:

SIR: I have the honor to report that, in accordance with your order of October 21, I proceeded with a part of my command, consisting of a part of the Thirty-fourth Ohio Mounted Infantry, a part of the Second (West) Virginia Cavalry Volunteers, and one section of Simmonds' battery, numbering in all about 300 men, toward Boone Court-House, W. Va., leaving Charleston at 7 p.m. of October 21.

In order to move my command with the greatest dispatch, Lieutenant-Colonel Shaw, commanding the Thirty-fourth Regiment, was ordered to cross his regiment on the ferry at Charleston and proceed to Camp Piatt, on the other side of the Kanawha, while I proceeded with the remainder of my force to Camp Piatt, and crossed by the ferry.

I reached Camp Piatt at 10 o'clock, and completed the crossing at 1:30 a.m. of October 22. About the same time I was joined by Colonel Shaw. Ascertaining that the country in which I was to operate was not favorable for the use of artillery, I left the section of Simmonds' battery at Camp Piatt.

Here I divided my command into three columns. I directed Major Hoffman, Second (West) Virginia Cavalry, to take command of the right column, consisting of 100 men, and Captain Allen, Second (West) Virginia Cavalry, to take command of the left column, consisting of 75 men, while I retained the main body under my own immediate command. Each column had a competent guide.

I directed Captain Allen to proceed by the right branch of Lens Creek across Big Coal, and thence to the road leading down the Pond Fork of Coal River, striking this road about 10 miles from the courthouse and proceeding down to the court-house. I directed Major Hoffman to proceed with the main body to a distance of 2 miles from the court-house; thence up Turtle Creek and across by way of Six-Mile Creek to the Spruce Fork of Coal River, coming down said creek and taking the town in the rear, while the main column I moved direct upon the court-house. These dispositions were such as to cut off all means of retreat from the enemy. The place was reached by the three columns at nearly the same time, between 12 and 3 o'clock of the 22d.

Having arrived at the place, I found no enemy except a few stragglers, who were captured by Major Hoffman and Captain Allen; also 1 man, Martin Snodgrass, of Company A, Thirteenth (West) Virginia Regiment (loyal), whom I suspect of being a deserter from the United States service, Major Hoffman, in capturing the stragglers, fired a few shots. I captured 3 horses.

I met with no loss, either in men or horses. I discovered that the information on which the movement was made was mainly without foundation, there having been at no time recently over 15 or 20 rebels at Boone Court-House, or over 150 in the whole country.

I ascertained that Colonel Beckley, with a few companies of a partly organized regiment of cavalry, was a few miles beyond Logan Court-House on Island Creek, but the distance being considerable, his way of retreat sure, and his having received information of our movement two or three days in advance, I determined not to attempt a movement against that force, being satisfied that it would be without any results worthy of mention.

The country through which I marched my command is rugged, the roads being scarcely passable for wagons in low water, and impracticable even for cavalry in high water. The supply of forage in very limited; very little hay is grown in all that country, and barely corn enough to subsist a part of the inhabitants.

I started back with my command on the morning of the 22d, and reached Camp Piatt at 5 p.m. of that day. I halted at Camp Piatt for the night, feeding and resting my horses, and brought them into camp on the morning of the 23d.

The distance marched was 80 miles; prisoners captured, 4; horses captured, 3.[319]

In the spring of 1864, violence intensified as large Union forces began concentrating in southern West Virginia to support General Grant's spring offensive in the east aimed at General Lee's army and the Confederate capital at Richmond. Joseph Harper, of Clear Fork of Coal River, had been sheriff of Fayette County during the 1840s and was a large landholder. Harper was noted for his kindness to the poor during the Civil War and made no distinction between Union and Confederate families. In April, he was taken from his home in the night by Confederate soldiers and murdered.[320]

In coordination with Union major general Franz Sigel's corps moving up the Shenandoah Valley, Brigadier General George Crook led more than six thousand Federal cavalry and infantry from West Virginia to cut the Virginia & Tennessee Railroad over the New River near Dublin, Virginia. Crook's sortie from Charleston was one of the largest Union raids of the war anywhere. The movement included Brigadier General William W. Averell with two thousand cavalry advancing through Boone, Wyoming and Logan Court Houses to destroy the saltworks at Saltville, Virginia. Averell's force was the largest to traverse the Coal River Valley during the war.

In a related action on May 29, a detachment of the Third West Virginia Cavalry and a body of Confederate guerrillas commanded by Captain John L. Chapman, of Lieutenant Colonel Vincent A. "Clawhammer" Witcher's Thirty-fourth Virginia Cavalry Battalion,

Brigadier General William W. Averell led a Union cavalry division through the Coal River Valley as part of Crook's raid against the Virginia and Tennessee Railroad in 1864. *Library of Congress.*

skirmished on the Curry farm, a quarter of a mile from Hamlin, in present-day Lincoln County. The Confederates on one side of the Mud River fired on a Federal detachment as it was proceeding up the river on the other side. The Union cavalry charged, and the Rebels retreated without loss. The fight resulted in one Federal killed and two wounded.[321]

In September 1864, Confederate raider Major James H. Nounnan, Sixteenth Virginia Cavalry Regiment, advanced from Tazewell, Virginia, and down the Coal River Valley to divert Federal attention from Witcher's raid through southern and central West Virginia. Nounnan's Confederate raiders emerged from the Coal River Valley and surprised the Seventh West

Virginia Cavalry Regiment in camp at Coalsmouth (St. Albans), seizing a considerable amount of supplies from a steamboat before they were driven away. Unable to cross the Kanawha, Nounnan's raiders in retiring rapidly from the valley collided with a body of Federals near Winfield. In a fierce mêlée, the Rebels were roughly handled and driven off.

The next month, another Confederate force advanced down the Coal River Valley. About 4:00 p.m. on October 21, 1864, Captain William Turner of the Raleigh County Scouts (Turner Home Guards), 184th Regiment, West Virginia State Troops, received intelligence that a Rebel force estimated at 440 cavalry and 50 infantry under Witcher was advancing via Forks of Coal in present-day Lincoln County. Turner, with 26 scouts from the counties of Kanawha, Raleigh, Wyoming and McDowell, took position in the Union fort at the fork. The remainder of his company was out on a scouting expedition. The firing was terrific both ways and lasted about one hour and twenty minutes. The Federals expended one thousand rounds. The Rebels succeeded in flanking the Federals and charged the fort. The Union men were compelled to abandon the fort or be captured. The next morning, the Federals divided into four squads and went to take positions near the road that the Rebels were expected to travel. The Federals ambushed the Rebels, who left three dead and continued to the Kanawha Valley. In the two-day action, Turner reported that the Rebels lost a total of 8 men dead and about 20 wounded.[322]

In the end, several thousand Coal River Valley men altogether served in the armies of the North and South in the Civil War. Nearly one thousand men altogether from Boone County alone served. While its contribution formed only a small part of the total West Virginia effort, on a per-capita basis, not many other counties provided more soldiers to the Union and Confederate armies, militia, Home Guards and West Virginia State Troops combined than Boone, which ranked among the highest per capita. Yet the men from this region who fought to preserve the Union or to establish the Confederacy and the roles they played in the Civil War have been largely forgotten. Today, a century and a half after the war's end, virtually no evidence of the foregoing events remains visible in the Coal River Valley—no statues, monuments, markers or plaques.[323] The forces that fought there were isolated from the war's larger theaters. And they were small—usually not larger than a regiment or battalion in size. Therefore, the region's saga in the Civil War never gained much lasting attention, and it became one of the least known.

Until now.

The commemoration of the Civil War's sesquicentennial has encouraged new looks at old historical assumptions, from scholars to the general public. Hopefully, this unique account has shed some needed light on the campaigning in the Coal River Valley in 1861 and how it fit into the pattern of the larger war of which it was part. This first interpretation of this small and dramatic, as well as important, series of operations concludes that making the Coal River Valley a contested buffer between the Raleigh-Wyoming-Logan line and the Kanawha Valley taught both sides the early importance in the mountains of small, fast-moving combat teams. The Coal River Valley was a proving ground for the economy of force strategy and tactics of raiding that effectively sustained the stranglehold over southern West Virginia and prevailed throughout the war.

Appendix A

BIOGRAPHIES

Following are brief biographies of people who figured prominently in the Civil War in the Coal River Valley operations in 1861 and afterward.

ADKINS, Cumberland (1822–after 1880). Union soldier. West Virginia. Farmer, deputy sheriff. Adkins was a staunch supporter of the Union cause. When war broke out, he was a leader in organizing the Peytona Home Guards militia for Union service. Adkins' company was active throughout 1861–62 and became part of the Eighth (West) Virginia Infantry Regiment.

ALLEN, James Henry. (1841–1919). Confederate officer. West Virginia. Private, 1862, First Cavalry Regiment, Virginia State Line; third lieutenant, Forty-fifth Virginia Cavalry Battalion. Allen was one of the "Immortal 600" Confederate prisoners of war placed under the shelling of friendly artillery fire at the siege of Charleston, South Carolina, in retaliation for the conditions of Union prisoners in Confederate prisons. They became famous throughout the South for refusing to take the oath of allegiance under such adverse circumstances.

BARKER, Joseph H. (1811–1880). Union officer. West Virginia. A staunch Union man, Barker was a leader in organizing the Peytona Home Guards militia for Union service with Barker's company and was active throughout 1861–62; captain, company commander, "Barker's Scouts," 1863, 1st Mounted Infantry Battalion, 187th Regiment, West Virginia State Troops

(Militia), Boone and Logan Counties; Second Lieutenant, November 30, 1863, 4th West Virginia Cavalry Regiment.

BECKLEY, Henry M. (1836–1868). Confederate officer. West Virginia. Captain, May 27, 1861, Company D, Thirty-sixth Virginia Infantry Regiment; colonel, May 15, 1862, First Virginia State Line Regiment; lieutenant colonel, April 4, 1863, Forty-fifth Virginia Infantry Battalion; captured September 19, 1864, Winchester, Virginia, and imprisoned at Fort Delaware, Delaware; released, oath of allegiance, June 8, 1865.

BIAS, William Van Buren. (1840–1903). Union officer. West Virginia. Methodist minister. Bias volunteered for the Peytona Home Guards militia as a private in Spurlock's company, July 10, 1861; enlisted in the Union army on September 2, 1861, Eighth (West) Virginia Infantry Regiment; promoted to sergeant, October 25, 1862; first lieutenant, Seventh West Virginia Cavalry, December 20, 1864. He served with distinction and was discharged on August 1, 1865, and became the first elected sheriff of Boone County. (Under the system prevailing before West Virginia became a separate state, the county sheriff and other county officers were appointed by the county court.)

BROUN, Thomas L. (1823–1914). Confederate officer. West Virginia. Lawyer, businessman. Before the war, he was associated with companies engaged in mining and shipping coal from the Coal River region. He succeeded Rosecrans as president of the Coal River Navigation Company, a position that he held until the beginning of the war in 1861. He entered the Confederate service in April 1861 as a private in the Twenty-second Virginia Infantry Regiment and was promoted to major in the fall of 1861, Sixtieth Virginia Infantry Regiment. During the summer of 1861, he led several hundred Boone and Logan Confederates in retreat from the Kanawha Valley via the Big Coal River region. After the war, he spent four years practicing law in New York City and returned to the position of president of the Coal River Navigation Company.

BUCHANAN, Thomas. (1821–1905). Union officer. West Virginia. Clerk of the Circuit Court of Logan County. Captain, company commander, 1863, 187th Regiment, West Virginia State Troops (Militia), Boone and Logan Counties; second lieutenant, August 29, 1863, 4th West Virginia Cavalry Regiment.

CHANDLER, William S. (1835–circa 1881). Confederate officer. West Virginia. Surveyor. Captain, company commander, June 1, 1861, Twenty-second Virginia Infantry Regiment (First Kanawha Regiment). During Floyd's autumn 1862 campaign, Chandler raised and led a company of Boone County volunteers (captain, company commander, "Chandler's Cavalry," September 17, 1862, Second Regiment, Virginia State Line Cavalry).

COOKE, Floyd (1820–1898). Union soldier. West Virginia. Farmer. Cooke came from Wyoming County in the 1840s and settled on the Boone County mountain that bears his family name (Cook Mountain.) His grandfathers were both Revolutionary War soldiers, and both were among the first settlers of Wyoming County. Cooke was a staunch supporter of the Union cause, and several of his sons served in the Union army during the Civil War. A justice of the peace, Cooke helped organize Union militia in the upper Pond Fork area. He and his father-in-law, William Walker Sr., built a small fort at Pond Fork for protection of the local Home Guards. Cooke fought at Boone Court House and Pond Fork. Captured at Bald Knob, he was sent to Libby Prison in Richmond for twenty-two months.

COX, Jacob D. (1828–1900). Union officer. Ohio. Lawyer, politician. Brigadier general, May 17, 1861; Kanawha Brigade, July 1, 1861–June 26, 1862; Kanawha Division, June 26–September 14, 1862; western Virginia, September 15, 1862–April 16, 1863; major general, October 6, 1862; afterward he commanded a division and later a corps under Sherman in the West. Cox was one of the war's most successful political generals.

COX, Thomas Jr. (1828–unknown). Union officer. Ohio. Captain, company commander, First Kentucky Infantry Regiment, June 5, 1861; commanded the Brownstown post in the Kanawha Valley under Guthrie; captured September 12, 1861, Coal River; imprisoned at Libby Prison in Richmond and later in Alabama, until exchanged in November 1862. During his imprisonment in the South, Cox earned distinction when he volunteered to substitute for an ill fellow prisoner selected for death in retaliation for the Union policy of executing captured guerrillas. The death sentence was commuted when the Union and Confederate governments agreed not to execute captured guerrillas.

DAVIS, James Lucius. (1813–1871). Confederate officer. Virginia. U.S. Army, 1854–61. Enlisted, Forty-sixth Virginia Infantry Regiment, June 6, 1861;

colonel, June 24, 1861; Tenth Virginia Cavalry Regiment, August 13, 1861; resigned February 2, 1865. Led Rebel forces at Coal River. Commanded a brigade under Stuart in 1864–65. Authored the Confederate army manual on cavalry tactics.

DAVIS, James Ward. (1819–1903). Confederate officer. West Virginia. Lawyer and politician, Greenbrier County. He entered the Confederate service in April 1861 as an aide to General Wise and was dispatched to command the militia in Wyoming, Logan and Boone Counties. Colonel. He commanded the Confederate force at Kanawha Gap, where he was severely wounded (a thumb and finger shot off, right arm broken and a gunshot wound in the breast). Captured and paroled, Davis saw no more active service. After the war, he returned to politics.

DUNBAR, William Sewell Dunbar. (1823–1898). Union officer. West Virginia. Carpenter, schoolteacher, physician. Captain, Company H, Eighth (West) Virginia Infantry Regiment, 1861; later the Seventh West Virginia Calvary Regiment; discharged in 1862 after the Battle of Cross Keys due to ill health; June 20, 1863, delegate of the first West Virginia state legislature; 1864–65, state senator at the second state legislature.

ELKINS, Daniel P. (1833–1906). Confederate officer. West Virginia. Second Lieutenant, June 1, 1861; first lieutenant, "Boone Rangers" cavalry, Twenty-second Virginia Infantry Regiment (First Kanawha Regiment), autumn 1861; captain, company commander, 1861–62, Thirty-sixth Virginia Infantry Regiment; captain, company commander, 1862, First Regiment, Virginia State Line; later captain, company commander, Forty-fifth Virginia Infantry Battalion ("Logan Wildcats").

ENYART, David A. (1826–1867). Union officer. Ohio. Lieutenant Colonel, First Kentucky Infantry Regiment, June 28, 1861; colonel, January 22, 1862; mustered out June 18, 1864. Led Federal forces at Red House, Boone Court House and the expedition to Raleigh Court House. Commanded a brigade under General Grant and later General Sherman in the West, advancing to brevet brigadier general, March 13, 1865.

FLOYD, John Buchanan. (1806–1863). Confederate officer. Virginia. Lawyer, planter, politician. U.S. secretary of war, 1857–60. Brigadier general, May 23, 1861; relieved, March 11, 1862; major general, Virginia

State Line, May 17, 1862–August 26, 1863. Commanded a brigade under Lee in western Virginia. General Floyd imagined a redoubt in the Boone-Logan region where thousands of Confederate diehards would winter 1861–62 in the rugged mountains, sustain themselves with local supplies and then attack the Federal army and retake the Kanawha Valley in the spring. He was a member of Congress for several terms and in 1850 became Virginia governor. He knew the Coal River Valley well, maintaining a hunting camp and a ginseng and peltry store in the upper Marshes of Coal until the late 1840s. He also bought cattle in this area. His brother in his early years lived in Raleigh County and settled in Logan County (now Mingo).

GRAMM, William. (1835–1888). Union officer. West Virginia. Second lieutenant, 1861–62, Peytona Home Guards militia; captain, 1863, West Virginia State Troops (Militia). Gramm reported the conditions in the Coal River Valley to the Federal army in the Kanawha Valley in the summer of 1861. He was captured and paroled in November 1862 while on a scouting mission along the Guyandotte River. He served with the Eighth (West) Virginia Infantry Regiment, later renamed the Seventh West Virginia Cavalry, and attained the rank of lieutenant colonel.

GUTHRIE, James V. (1809–1896). Union officer. Ohio. Lawyer, politician. Colonel, First Kentucky Infantry Regiment, June 4, 1861; resigned, December 1861. Commanded the Charleston district in the Kanawha Valley under Cox, August–December 1861.

HARLESS, Cumberland. (1834–1883). Union soldier. West Virginia. Peytona Home Guards militia, 1861; captain, company commander, 1862, 187th Regiment, West Virginia State Troops (Militia), Boone County; 1863, corporal, later private, 7th West Virginia Cavalry Regiment. As Confederate forces under Colonel Ezekiel Miller assembled at Boone Court House, concern grew at General Cox's headquarters in the Kanawha Valley about the state of affairs and the pro-Union people in the Coal River Valley. The capture and imprisonment of Harless in the Boone County jail in August 1861 by the Rebel militia triggered Cox's decision to invade.

HATFIELD, William A. "Devil Anse" (1839–1921). Confederate officer. West Virginia. Logger. Fought with the 129th Virginia Militia Regiment (Logan), 1861; captain, Virginia State Line, 1862–63; first lieutenant, 45th Virginia Infantry Battalion, April 1863–February 1864; as a guerrilla captain led a unit called the Logan Wildcats that was active in Boone, Logan and Wyoming Counties, 1864–65. Believed to have fought with Confederate forces at Red House, Boone Court House and Kanawha Gap. Later after the war, he was the leader of the Hatfield clan in the famous Hatfield-McCoy feud.

LEWIS, PRYCE (1828–1911). Federal spy. Born in 1828 in Wales, Lewis immigrated to the United States in 1856. He was employed by the Pinkerton Detective Agency and worked as a spy for the Union in Richmond. Intelligence gathered by Lewis in the Kanawha Valley region in the summer of 1861, including his escape back to Union lines via Boone County, helped the Union army gain control of the region. Later in the war, he was captured and sentenced to be hanged but escaped death because of his British citizenship. After his release, he served as bailiff and special detective officer of the Old Capitol Prison in Washington, D.C., until the end of the war. Lewis is regarded as one the Civil War's most daring spies. He committed suicide by jumping from the top of New York's Pulitzer Building in 1911.

McSHERRY, James W. (1833–1930). Confederate officer. West Virginia. Physician. Captain, company commander, "Boone Rangers," June 1, 1861, Thirty-sixth Virginia Infantry Regiment (Second Kanawha Regiment). He served on the staff of General John McCausland and participated in the 1861 West Virginia campaign, in Kentucky with General Floyd's command and, later, served with General Joseph E. Johnston at Chattanooga and Knoxville. Wounded at Carnifex Ferry and Fort Donelson, McSherry was captured in Boone County in 1864 and imprisoned at Fort Delaware until the war's end. After the war, he was a longtime member of the city council and twice mayor of Martinsburg. McSherry's wife, Virginia Faulkner McSherry, was president general of the United Daughters of the Confederacy from 1900 to 1911. His brother-in-law was former U.S. representative and minister to France Charles J. Faulkner, who became a Confederate lieutenant colonel and "Stonewall" Jackson's chief of staff.

MILLER, Ezekiel S. (1813–1875). Confederate officer. West Virginia. Farmer, magistrate. Colonel, 187th Virginia Militia Regiment (Boone); organized and led the initial Confederate defense of the Coal River Valley, summer 1861; led Confederate forces in attack on Union force at Red House; commanded the Confederate forces against the Union assault on Boone Court House and the Boone detachment of Confederates under James Ward Davis at Kanawha Gap.

PATE, Henry Clay (1832–1864). Confederate officer. West Virginia. Lawyer, publisher. Son of the founder and president of the prewar Coal River Navigation Company, based in Peytona. Leader of the pro-slavery Missourians ("Border Ruffians") and the captive of John Brown at Black Jack in Kansas in 1856. Captain, Petersburg Rangers, June 5, 1861–May 25, 1862; lieutenant colonel, Second Virginia Cavalry Battalion, May 25, 1862; lieutenant colonel, Fifth Virginia Cavalry Regiment, under J.E.B. Stuart's command, June 23, 1862; colonel, Fifth Virginia Cavalry Regiment, September 28, 1863; killed at Yellow Tavern, Virginia, on May 11, 1864, while making a desperate stand against Union general Phil Sheridan.

PIATT, Abraham Sanders (1821–1908). Federal officer. Ohio. Publisher. Colonel, Thirteenth Ohio Infantry Regiment, April 20, 1861; mustered out three months later; raised the Thirty-fourth Ohio Infantry Regiment, that state's first Zouave regiment; colonel, September 2, 1861; brigadier general, April 28, 1862; resigned from service February 17, 1863; went into politics and later wrote poetry. Commanded the Union forces at Kanawha Gap.

SCRAGG, Samuel (1820–1906). Union soldier. West Virginia. Born in England, Scragg was foreman at the Peytona Mines. In public meetings of citizens during 1861, he actively urged people to support the Union and encouraged formation of the Peytona Home Guards. In August, he was among the Peytona Home Guards arrested by the Confederate militia based at Boone Court House and jailed. Allowed to escape by a sympathetic guard, he crossed the mountains to reach the Union camp at Brownstown and reported the conditions in the Coal River Valley to the Federals. As a guide, he accompanied the Union force that burned Boone Court House. He served with the Seventh West Virginia Cavalry Regiment.

SIMMONDS, Seth J. (circa 1821–after 1890). Union officer. Ohio. Mustered in and elected captain of Simmonds' battery, Kentucky Light Artillery, July 15, 1861; commanded sections at Boone Court House, Coal River and Kanawha Gap; served with distinction at Antietam, September 1862; later served in the West with Sherman; cashiered, March 1864.

SPURLOCK, John. (1819–1907). Union officer. West Virginia. Peytona Home Guards militia, 1861; captain, company commander, 1862–63, 187th Regiment, West Virginia State Troops, Boone County; 1863, private, 7th West Virginia Cavalry Regiment.

STOLLINGS, Joel E. (1833–1897). Confederate officer. West Virginia. Lawyer, merchant, politician. Captain, company commander, 1861, 187th Virginia Militia Regiment (Boone); deputy commander, Confederate defense of Boone Court House; believed to have fought with Boone militia detachment of Confederates under James Ward Davis at Kanawha Gap; first lieutenant, 1862, Chandler's Cavalry, 2nd Virginia State Line; captain, company commander, 1863, 45th Virginia Infantry Battalion. Captured with his company at Abb's Valley, Virginia, by Toland during the Virginia & Tennessee Railroad raid (1864). After the war, Stollings became a member of West Virginia state senate. He was one of the leading men of Boone County and was very wealthy.

TOLAND, John T. (1826–1863). Union officer. Ohio. Sold dental goods in Cincinnati before the war. He assisted Piatt in organizing the Thirty-fourth Ohio Infantry Regiment; was appointed lieutenant colonel on August 2, 1861, and colonel on May 14, 1862. In September 1862, at Fayette Court House, Toland had three horses shot from under him but was uninjured. After the Federal retreat from the Kanawha Valley, he commanded a brigade in Gilmore's division, leading the advance that resulted in driving the Rebels from the valley. In July 1863, commanding a mounted brigade, he was assigned to destroy the Virginia & Tennessee Railroad. He was killed in battle at Wytheville, Virginia, on July 18, at the head of his command on horseback when he was shot. Toland distinguished himself at Kanawha Gap.

TONEY, John Poindexter, Jr. (1830–1908). Confederate officer. West Virginia. Boatsman. First lieutenant, June 20, 1861, Twenty-second Virginia Infantry Regiment; captain, company commander, March 1, 1862; captured November 6, 1863, at Droop Mountain; imprisoned November 18, 1863, at Camp Chase, Ohio; March 2, 1864, at Fort Delaware; released June 12, 1865.

VANDELINDE, George A. "Doc" (1813–1867). Confederate officer. Surgeon. West Virginia. Farmer, physician. Born in the Netherlands, he immigrated to the United States before 1842. Veteran of the Belgian Revolution (1830–32), he served as surgeon, 187th Virginia Militia Regiment (Boone), 1861, and tended Confederate and Union wounded at Boone Court House and Kanawha Gap. Captured at Kanawha Gap, he took the oath of allegiance and was paroled. Purportedly, owing to his good nature toward others and the medical care he provided to both sides, "Doc" Vandelinde's homestead and lands were unmolested throughout the war. Assayer, artist, poet.

VIA, Jackson (circa 1829–unknown). Confederate soldier. West Virginia. Schoolteacher. In May 1861, commissioned second lieutenant in Company D, Thirty-sixth Virginia Infantry Regiment at Peytona; May 27, 1862, promoted to first lieutenant. He served throughout the war, commanding Company B after Captain James W. McSherry was captured in Boone County in early 1864. Captured at Waynesboro, Virginia, on March 2, 1865, and sent to Fort Delaware. Released on June 17, 1865.

WALKER, William, Jr. (1826–1899). Union officer. West Virginia. Farmer, pastor, teacher, lawyer. Walker helped organize Union militia in Wyoming County, commanding a company of the 190th Virginia (Wyoming) Militia Regiment. He represented Wyoming County in the West Virginia Constitutional Convention of 1861 and served with the Seventh West Virginia Cavalry Regiment.

WALKER, William, Sr. (1799–1883). Union officer. West Virginia. Farmer, pastor. Walker, a respected member of the community, assisted in organizing several prewar churches in the area. Staunchly pro-Union, he cast the only vote for Abraham Lincoln in Boone County in 1860. At the outbreak of the war, he helped organize Union militia in Boone County. Along with son-in-law Floyd Cooke and others, he constructed a fort at Walnut Gap for protection against Confederate raiders and Home Guards. Captured in Pate's attack at Pond Fork, Walker was released owing to his advanced age.

WHITE, Micajah Goodwin. (1810–1883). Union soldier. West Virginia. Miller by trade. Prior to the Civil War, White lived on Upper Pond Fork of the Little Coal River. A Union man, White volunteered to serve in Barker's company, Peytona Home Guards, in the summer of 1861. He fought at Boone Court House, and oral tradition suggests that he and another Union militia man set the fire that burned the courthouse. White was captured at Bald Knob and sent to Libby Prison in Richmond. Imprisoned twenty-two months, he afterward served with the 187th Regiment, West Virginia State Troops. Four of his sons also served in the Union army, and the two eldest were killed.

WISE, Henry A. (1806–1876). Confederate officer. Virginia. Lawyer, politician. Prewar governor of Virginia. Brigadier general, June 5, 1861; commanded brigade ("Wise's Legion") in western Virginia, June–September 1861. Wise dispatched his cavalry under James Lucius Davis to the Coal River Valley to counter Union raiding and avenge the burning of Boone Court House. In the summer of 1861, Wise and General John B. Floyd began feuding over who was the ranking commander in western Virginia. Floyd blamed Wise for the Confederate loss at the Battle of Carnifex Ferry for refusing to come to his aid. President Jefferson Davis removed Wise from his command in western Virginia. Wise commanded Rebel forces in the Battle of Roanoke Island and a brigade during the Seven Days Battles (1862). For the rest of 1862 and 1863, he held various commands in North Carolina and Virginia. In 1864, Wise commanded a brigade defending Petersburg and was credited with saving the city in the First Battle of Petersburg and, to an extent, the Second Battle of Petersburg. He led a brigade in the Army of Northern Virginia during the siege of Petersburg and was promoted to major general after the Battle of Sayler's Creek, Virginia. He was with General Robert E. Lee at Appomattox Court House.

WORKMAN, William Jesse. (1821–1904). Union soldier. West Virginia. Farmer. In the summer of 1861, Workman, son of a War of 1812 hero and frontiersman, established contact with Cox in the Kanawha Valley on behalf of Unionists in Boone County. Slipping back and forth between the lines, Workman performed as a Union scout and guide. He helped organize Union militia in the upper Pond Fork area and served with the Peytona Home Guards and Eighth (West) Virginia Infantry. Workman fought at Boone Court House and was with the Federal force that was defeated at Coal River, afterward escaping to Peytona. Workman was captured at Bald Knob and sent to Libby Prison in Richmond and then Salisbury (North Carolina) Prison. Imprisoned a total of eighteen months, he served with the Seventh West Virginia Cavalry Regiment after his release.

Appendix B

CASUALTIES

Action	Date	UNION			
		Killed	**Wounded**	**Captured**	**Civilians**
Forks of Coal (a)	August	—	—	—	—
Peytona (b)	August	—	—	3	—
Bald Knob (c)	August	—	—	—	2
Pond Fork (d)	August	—	—	—	—
Spruce Fork (e)	August	—	—	—	6
Red House (f)	August 31	—	—	—	—
Boone Court House (g)	September 1	2	9	—	—
Coal River (h)	September 12	5	4	49	—
Big Coal River (i)	September 13	—	—	—	—
Pond Fork (j)	September 17	—	1	3	—
Bald Knob (k)	September 18	—	—	14	—
Kanawha Gap (l)	September 25–26	4	8	—	—
Total	**August–September**	**11**	**22**	**69**	**8**

Appendix B

Action	Date	Killed	Wounded	Captured	Civilians
		CONFEDERATE			
Forks of Coal (a)	August	—	—	2	—
Peytona (b)	August	1	—	—	—
Bald Knob (c)	August	—	—	—	—
Pond Fork (d)	August	—	—	2	—
Spruce Fork (e)	August	—	—	—	—
Red House (f)	August 31	1	2	6	—
Boone Court House (g)	September 1	1	7	5	35
Coal River (h)	September 12	—	1	—	17
Big Coal River (i)	September 13–15	—	—	—	35
Pond Fork (j)	September 17	—	—	—	—
Bald Knob (k)	September 18	—	—	—	—
Kanawha Gap (l)	September 25-26	2	3	50	—
Total	**August–September**	**5**	**13**	**65**	**87**

	Killed	Wounded	Captured	Civilians	Total
Union	11	22	69	8	110
Confederate	5	13	65	87	170
Total	**16**	**35**	**134**	**95**	**280**

a. Forks of Coal (Union scouting expedition)

b. Peytona (Confederate militia operations)

c. Bald Knob (Confederate militia operations)

d. Pond Fork (Union militia operations)

e. Spruce Fork (Confederate militia operations)

f. Red House (Battle)

g. Boone Court House (Battle)

h. Coal River (Battle)

i. Big Coal River—(Union raid)

j. Pond Fork—(Battle)

k. Bald Knob—(Confederate raid)

l. Kanawha Gap—(Battle)

Notes

Introduction

1. Oral tradition (hereafter OT), Roush.
2. Twain, *Writings of Mark Twain*, 118.
3. Hacker, "A Census-Based Count of the Civil War Dead," 307–48. The 620,000 men referred to here may be found in the widely used synthesis McPherson, *Battle Cry of Freedom*, 854.
4. Phisterer, *Statistical Record*, 64.
5. Vargo, "Little Coal River Improvement Project," 1; Forbes, "John Peter Salling."
6. Currey, "The Coal River," 9.
7. Krebs, Teets and White, *West Virginia Geological Survey*, 9.
8. Dean, *Coal, Steamboats, Timber and Trains*.
9. Summers, *Mountain State*, 123–24.
10. Floyd Cooke (1820–1898) was the last of his line to spell the surname with an "e" at the end. His children's surname was shortened to Cook.
11. Creasey, *Fifteen Decisive Battles*, ix.

Chapter 1

12. Snell, *West Virginia and the Civil War*.
13. The name "Army of Western Virginia" is often given to the Union force that fought under McClellan, but it was not called that until the *New York Times* (July 23, 1861) ran an article announcing McClellan's departure to command the Army of the Potomac on this date.

14. McClellan, *McClellan's Own Story*.
15. Snell, *West Virginia and the Civil War*, 17–40.
16. Cox, *Military Reminiscences*, 1: 43.
17. Lowry, *Battle of Scary Creek*.
18. Ibid., 92–98.
19. Evans, *Confederate Military History*, 159.
20. Wood, *Raleigh County*, 126; Journey Up Coal River, "History of Coal River Part 1."
21. Hoeft, "A Colorful History," 24.
22. Evans, *Confederate Military History*, 37.
23. Lewis, *Pioneers of the Virginias*, 13.
24. Linger, *Confederate Military Units*.
25. *Louisville Courier*, September 6, 1861; *Cincinnati Daily Press*, September 13, 1861.
26. U.S. War Department, *A Compilation of the Official Records*, Series 2, 2:1450, hereafter referred to as *OR*.
27. Stutler, *West Virginia in the Civil War*, 162.
28. Haga, "Civil War Journal of William Sewell Dunbar."
29. Ibid.
30. Catton, *Coming Fury*, 352.
31. Stutler, *West Virginia in the Civil War*, 304.
32. Lewis, *Pioneers of the Virginias*, 352.
33. West Virginia Division of Culture and History, "Debates and Proceedings: December 4, 1861."
34. Lewis, *Pioneers of the Virginias*, 352.
35. Bullard, "1890 Veterans Census"; White, *First Biennial Message of Governor Albert B. White*; West Virginia Department of Archives and History, *West Virginia History, Volumes 56–58*, 124.
36. Lewis, *Pioneers of the Virginias*, 13.
37. Linger, *Confederate Military Units*; Wallace, *Guide to Virginia Military Organizations*.
38. *Rolla Express*, September 9, 1861.
39. Hatfield, *The Other Feud*, 14.
40. Hoeft, "A Colorful History," 23.
41. Virginia Board of Public Works, *Annual Report...Vol. 36*.
42. Peyton, *Memoir*, 231–34.
43. Hufford, interview with Howard Miller.
44. *Charleston Gazette*, July 18, 1948. Also known as Coon's Mills, Coons Mill, Coon Mill and Coons Mills.
45. Keegan, *History of Warfare*, 244–46. Keegan's observations about the perspectives of warfare of the ancient Greeks, also mountainous people, aptly apply to the history of war in southern West Virginia.

46. *Kith and Kin of Boone County*, Vol. XVIII, No. 3, and Vol. XX, No. 1.

47. Database of Virginia Military Dead, "Morris, Fenell."

48. Haga, "Civil War Journal of William Sewell Dunbar."

49. Cushing, *Story of Our Post Office*, 481.

50. Hager, *Blue and Grey Battlefields*, 9. The correct spelling is Scragg, without an "s" at the end.

51. "Robert Hager," Biographies of West Virginia Statehood Leaders. Prepared by Marshall University Humanities Program graduate students enrolled in Dr. Billy Joe Peyton's Fall 2010 "Historical Studies" class at Marshall's South Charleston campus, http://www.wvculture.org/history/sesquicentennial/hagerrobert.pdf; Hager, *Boone County, West Virginia History*.

52. *Wheeling Intelligencer*, "The First West Virginia Legislature."

53. Hager, *Boone County, West Virginia History*.

54. C. Stratton letter from Peytona, Boone County, Virginia, June 20, 1862.

55. Lang, *Loyal West Virginia*; Bullard, "1890 Veterans Census."

56. *OR*, Series 2, 2:1451.

57. Ibid.

58. Ibid.

59. Haga, "Civil War Journal of William Sewell Dunbar."

60. OT, Chumley.

61. OT, Chumley and Miller.

62. Stutler, *West Virginia in the Civil War*, 163.

63. *Richmond Times Dispatch*, September 9, 1861; *Tazewell (VA) Democrat*, September 14, 1861; *Daily Nashville Patriot* "Boon Courthouse, Va. Burnt by Federal Scoundrels."

64. *OR*, Series 2, 2:1450–51.

65. Evans, *Confederate Military History*, 37.

66. *Daily Nashville Patriot*, "Boon Courthouse, Va. Burnt by Federal Scoundrels."

67. *Compiled*, 1,532–33; Hill, *26th Ohio Veteran Volunteer Infantry*, 52.

68. Cox, *Military Reminiscences*, 63.

69. *New York Times*, "The Fight at Boone Court-House"; *Cincinnati Gazette*, September 5, 1861.

70. *OR*, 51: 273.

71. Cox, *Military Reminiscences*, 99.

CHAPTER 2

72. The village is described in the 1835–57 editions of the *Virginia Gazetteer*; *Charleston Daily Mail*, May 19, 1929.

73. Callahan, *History of West Virginia*, 1:81–93.
74. Hill, *26ᵗʰ Ohio Veteran Volunteer Infantry*, 2.
75. *Gallipolis Journal*, "Details of the Boone Court House Fight"; Dyer, *Compendium of the War of the Rebellion*. Although credited to Kentucky's levy of volunteers for the Union armies, the First Kentucky Infantry and Light Artillery had been raised in Ohio. Kelly, *Historic Sketch*, 4, states that the Twenty-sixth Ohio's Company E also participated in the Boone Court House expedition, but to this date, no other supporting sources have been found. The company might have formed part of the reserve force with the Fourth (West) Virginia's companies.
76. Hewett, *Supplement to the Official Records*, Part 2, 51:726.
77. Hager, *Blue and Grey Battlefields*, 9–10.
78. Hill, *26ᵗʰ Ohio Veteran Volunteer Infantry*, 52. Ironically, Company K was composed primarily of soldiers from Madison County, Ohio. After the war, Boone Court House was renamed Madison, after a lawyer who had been instrumental in the creation of Boone County in 1847.
79. *Cleveland Morning Leader*, "Late from the Kanawha."
80. Deasy. For information on the "Deasy" spelling, see National Park Service, "Civil War Soldiers and Sailors."
81. Stutler, *West Virginia in the Civil War*, 162–63.
82. Ibid., 163.
83. The *Richmond Times Dispatch*, September 11, 1861, puts the Confederate strength at Boone Court House at "about two hundred fighting an army of near 1,200." Hill, *26ᵗʰ Ohio Veteran Volunteer Infantry*, 52, puts the Confederate strength at 220; Stutler, *West Virginia in the Civil War*, 163, at "between three and four hundred untrained militiamen." Captain William Baisden, company commander, 129ᵗʰ Regiment (Logan), reported 225 militia (*Compiled Records*, Virginia reel, 298). Other estimates from the time run as high as 450 and 600, which are considered too high.
84. *Richmond Times Dispatch*, September 11, 1861.
85. Hatfield, *The Other Feud*, 13–14.
86. Ibid. Although open to debate since no supporting documentation has been discovered, the long-standing traditional view is that Hatfield fought at Boone Court House with the Boone-Logan militia.
87. Hager, *Blue and Grey Battlefields*, 10.
88. *Compiled Records*, Ohio reel, 1,537.
89. Ibid.; *Cincinnati Gazette*, September 5, 1861; *New York Times*, September 8, 1861; *Gallipolis Journal*, September 12, 1861; Moore, *Rebellion Record*, 12; *Richmond Times Dispatch*, September 11, 1861.
90. *Richmond Times Dispatch*, September 9, 1861.
91. Hill, *26ᵗʰ Ohio Veteran Volunteer Infantry*, 52.
92. Hager, *Blue and Grey Battlefields*, 10–11.

93. National Park Service, "Civil War Soldiers and Sailors."

94. Lewis, *Pioneers of the Virginias*, 13.

95. Deasy.

96. *Gallipolis Journal*, September 12, 1861.

97. Deasy.

98. *Gallipolis Journal*, September 12, 1861. Re: James W. Nowlin, see National Park Service, "Civil War Soldiers and Sailors."

99. Lewis, *Pioneers of the Virginias*, 13.

100. *OR*, 5:122–25; Ibid., 51:472.

101. Hewett, *Supplement to the Official Records*, Part 2, 51:727.

102. *Richmond Times Dispatch*, September 11, 1861. The report provided to state militia general Augustus A. Chapman, which he reported to General Floyd, placed the number of Union troops at eight hundred (*OR*, Part 2, 51:273).

103. *Gallipolis Journal*, September 12, 1861. "F.F.V." was an acronym for "First Families of Virginia."

104. Deasy.

105. National Park Service, "Civil War Soldiers and Sailors."

106. OT, Chumley.

107. Callahan, *History of West Virginia*, 3:349.

108. Cox, *Military Reminiscences*, 161–62.

109. *OR*, Series 2, 2:1,450; Callahan, *History of West Virginia*, 3:119.

110. Hale, *History of the Great Kanawha Valley*, 1:110.

111. *Gallipolis Journal*, September 12, 1861; Stutler, *West Virginia in the Civil War*, 147; Hill, *26ʰ Ohio Veteran Volunteer Infantry*, 678.

112. Hager, *Blue and Grey Battlefields*, 10. There is an oral tradition that the Boone County Courthouse was burned by two men by the name of White and Whitt (also spelled as Whit), surnames historically associated with the Pond Fork and upper Wyoming County area (OT; Price, "Courthouse Burning.") In fact, two Whites served in Captain Joseph H. Barker's Union militia company: Private Micajah White, a prominent pro-Union man in Boone County, and one of his four sons, Private Benjamin White. Meanwhile, Private Edley (Audley) Whit served in Captain William Walker's Union Home Guard (Wyoming) company of the 190ʰ (West) Virginia Militia and later in Captain Shorten Smith's company (McDowell) (Blankenship, "Heinous Deed of 1863 Recalled.") In addition, Stutler, *West Virginia in the Civil War*, 147, reports that Confederate militiaman Private Robert Whitt (Whit) was captured.

113. Stutler, *West Virginia in the Civil War*, 147.

114. *Daily Nashville Patriot*, "Boon Courthouse, Va. Burnt by Federal Scoundrels"; *Civilian and Gazette Weekly*, October 15, 1861.

115. Hager, *Blue and Grey Battlefields*, 10. Most county records that were recorded prior to that time (i.e., birth, death, marriage, land and probate) were lost.

116. *Raleigh Register*, "Boone and Logan Court Houses Burned."

117. *Fremont Journal*, "The Fight at Boone Court House"; *Gallipolis Journal*, September 12, 1861, citing a letter report by First Lieutenant Joseph H. Ross, Company G, Twenty-sixth Ohio.

118. *Annual Cyclopedia and Register*, 377; Sahr, "Inflation Conversion Factors."

119. Lewis, *Pioneers of the Virginias*, 13.

120. Stutler, "Boone and Logan Court Houses Burned," differs somewhat from the chapter of the same title in Stutler's *West Virginia in the Civil War*.

121. Hewett, *Supplement to the Official Records*, Part 2, 51:727.

122. *OR*, 5:840; *Richmond Times Dispatch*, September 11, 1861.

123. Cox, *Military Reminiscences of the Civil War*, 99.

124. Stutler, *West Virginia in the Civil War*, 163.

125. *Annual Cyclopedia and Register*, 72, 741. This number, however high the estimate, is not implausible if the capture of the town's citizens are assumed.

126. National Park Service, "Civil War Soldiers and Sailors."

127. *New York Times*, "The Fight at Boone Court-House"; *Cincinnati Gazette*, September 5, 1861.

128. *OR*, 51:468.

129. Ross report cited in *Fremont Journal*, "The Fight at Boone Court House"; National Park Service, "Civil War Soldiers and Sailors."

130. Long, "Army Correspondence," dated September 5, 1861.

131. *Cincinnati Gazette*, September 5, 1861; *New York Times*, September 8, 1861; *Gallipolis Journal*, September 12, 1861; Moore, *Rebellion Record*, 12; *Richmond Times Dispatch*, September 11, 1861.

132. *American and Commercial Advertiser* "Fight Between Union Men and Secessionists at Boone Court House."

133. *New York Herald*, "Battle at Boone Court House"; *New York Sun*, "Another Victory in Western Virginia"; *New York Times*, "Another Victory of the National Troops."

134. Victor, *History…of the Southern Rebellion*, 2:222.

135. Rees and Rees, *Chronological History of the Great Rebellion*, 17.

136. Cooper, *Chronological and Alphabetical Record*, 62, 74.

137. Denison, *Winfield Scott*, 106–07.

138. *Tazewell (VA) Democrat*, September 14, 1861; *Daily Nashville Patriot*, "Boon Courthouse, Va. Burnt by Federal Scoundrels."

139. *Raleigh Register*, May 25, 1959.

140. Ibid.

141. OT, Chumley.

142. *Richmond Times Dispatch*, September 11, 1861.

143. U.S. Census Bureau, "U.S. Census Population Schedule, 1860."

144. Guerci, "It Took a War."

145. Cox, *Military Reminiscences*, 161–62.

146. *OR*, Series 2, 2:1,450.

147. Newman, *Smoots of Maryland and Virginia*, 152–62; Olafson, "The Smoot Family of Boone County, West Virginia"; Boone County, (West) Virginia 1860 Federal Census.

148. West Virginia: The Other History, "Camp Chase Civil Prisoners"; Boone County Genealogical Society, *Kith and Kin of Boone County*.

149. Noe, "Exterminating Savages," in *The Civil War in Appalachia*, 115.

150. Deasy. The war in western Virginia was especially vicious as both sides killed prisoners, and the Coal River Valley was no exception. Given the large number of murders and reprisals known for this region during the war, Deasy's testimony of cold-blooded killings is not surprising, and while it does not prove it happened in this campaign, his report is significant nonetheless. As one of the important leading members of the postwar Catholic laity in Ohio, his reputation as a historical source is difficult to discount (Carr, "Timothy H. Deasy," 128).

151. *Richmond Times Dispatch*, September 11, 1861.

152. *Organization Index to Pension Files of Veterans Who Served Between 1861 and 1900*, "Nowlen, James W."

153. *Official Roster of Soldiers of the State of Ohio*, 3:250; Casey, "Descendants of William Mullins and Katheryn Smith/Smythe; Hill, *26ᵗʰ Ohio Veteran Volunteer Infantry*, 53; Allen et al, *Kith and Kin of Boone County*.

154. Hill, *26ᵗʰ Ohio Veteran Volunteer Infantry*, 53.

155. Kentucky Adjutant General's Office, *Report, 1861–1866*, 1:527.

156. West Virginia State Library, History and Archives, "Virgil A. Lewis," http://www.wvculture.org/history/wvsamenu.html.

157. Turner, *7ᵗʰ West Virginia Cavalry*, 90. In addition, Turner (p. 135) also reports that Private David Williams was "wounded by guerrillas near Madison, WV before entering service (3 Nov 1861 Wyoming Co. VA)." Williams was one of seven brothers who served in the Union army.

158. *Compiled Records*, Virginia reel, 298.

159. *Tazewell (VA) Democrat*, September 14, 1861; *Daily Nashville Patriot*, "Boon Courthouse, Va. Burnt by Federal Scoundrels."

160. Dilger and White, "Boone County History."

161. Livermore, *Numbers and Losses*.

162. To be sure, historical citations of the Battle of Boone Court House differ widely in estimating the total number of Confederate casualties. Yet another period source, the *American Annual Cyclopedia and Register of Important Events of the Year 1861*, places the number of Confederate casualties at "30 killed, a large number wounded, and forty prisoners taken" (p. 72). Assuming the most commonly cited numbers—(a) 40 total military and civilian captured, including (b) 5 soldiers—and applying (c)

Livermore's rule of 1:2.5 ratio of killed to wounded results in an estimate of 20 Confederate military casualties, including 4 killed and mortally wounded, 11 wounded and 5 captured. Adding 35 civilians and slaves taken prisoner makes for a total Southern loss of 55, a reasonable estimate. Interestingly, assuming the historical rates of fire and range of weapons used at Boone Court House, factored for the number of troops engaged and the duration of the action, adjusted for the effects of untrained militia, yields an estimate of 6 Confederate dead and 14 wounded; and 5 Union dead and 12 wounded. It is highly unlikely, therefore, that the Rebels suffered from the fire of the Union militia but did not themselves inflict casualties on the exposed Union militia, which bore the brunt of the fight for the Federals. Thus, a reasonable conservative estimate of Union militia casualties, statistically arrived at, would be 3 dead and 5 wounded, exploding the implausible supposition that the only Union casualties were suffered by the Twenty-sixth Ohio and First Kentucky volunteers.

163. West Virginia Division of Culture and History, "Debates and Proceedings: December 4, 1861."

164. *Civilian and Gazette Weekly*, October 15, 1861.

165. OT, Chumley. Chumley's grandfather Vernon G. Vandelinde (1854–1935) observed the Federal column returning to the Kanawha Valley. The *Gallipolis Journal*'s September 5, 1861 report called the Union force "a scouting party."

166. The destructive flooding of autumn 1861 throughout western Virginia also contributed to the distress and famine that followed. The deadly flooding swept away homes, families and communities.

167. *Gallipolis Journal*, September 12, 1861.

168. Bullard, "1890 Veterans Census."

169. Hayes, Horan and Williams, "William Van Buren Bias and Descendants," in *Kith and Kin of Boone County*.

170. Turner, *7th West Virginia Cavalry*, 1.

171. Hewett, *Supplement to the Official Records*, Part 2, 51:727.

172. Hill, *26th Ohio Veteran Volunteer Infantry*, 56.

173. *Daily Ohio Statesman*, November 17, 1861.

174. Denison, *Winfield Scott*, 106–07.

175. Hayward, *Poetical Pen-Pictures*, 112–13.

176. *OR*, Series 2, 2:870.

CHAPTER 3

173. Cox, *Military Reminiscences*, 99.

178. The Union order of battle for the Battle of Coal River is determined by matching the First Kentucky Infantry Regiment companies to the names

of the forty-seven Federal soldiers "recently captured by the First Virginia Cavalry, under Colonel J.L. Davis, on Cole river in Boone county" (Jeffrey, *Richmond Prisons*, 227–30); National Park Service, "Civil War Soldiers and Sailors"; Speed et al, *Union Regiments of Kentucky*.

179. *Richmond Times Dispatch*, October 7, 1861.

180. *Nashville Union and American*, "From Wise's Legion."

181. *OR*, Part 1, 5:839.

182. "The Rockbridge Rangers," Court Minutes, 1898–1903; Rockbridge County Court, Virginia. Rockbridge County, Va., 26–27; National Park Service, "Civil War Soldiers and Sailors System."

183. *Nashville Union and American*, "From Wise's Legion."

184. Davis report of skirmish at Toney Creek in Hewett, *Supplement to the Official Records*, Part 1, 1:377–78.

185. *Nashville Union and American*, "From Wise's Legion."

186. Ibid.

187. While the October 7, 1861 *Richmond Times Dispatch* cited that the Confederates crossed the Coal River ninety-seven times, Colonel Davis cited ninety-two times in his report.

188. *Richmond Times Dispatch*, September 25, 1861.

189. *Nashville Union and American*, "From Wise's Legion."

190. *Richmond Times Dispatch*, September 25, 1861.

191. *Nashville Union and American*, "From Wise's Legion."

192. *Richmond Times Dispatch*, September 25, 1861.

193. *Richmond Dispatch*, May 24, 1861.

194. *Nashville Union and American*, "From Wise's Legion."

195. Ibid.

196. *Richmond Times Dispatch*, September 25, 1861.

197. Ibid.

198. *Nashville Union and American*, "From Wise's Legion."

199. *Richmond Times Dispatch*, September 25, 1861.

200. *Nashville Union and American*, "From Wise's Legion."

201. *Richmond Times Dispatch*, October 7, 1861.

202. Ibid.

203. *Nashville Union and American*, "From Wise's Legion." This source reports the Rebels attacked with 150 to 175 cavalry.

204. *Richmond Dispatch*, September 25, 1861.

205. *Nashville Union and American*, "From Wise's Legion."

206. *Richmond Dispatch*, September 25, 1861.

207. Jeffrey, *Richmond Prisons*, 227–30.

208. *Richmond Dispatch*, September 25, 1861.

209. National Park Service, "Civil War Soldiers and Sailors"; *Cincinnati Daily Press*, "Battle of John's Run." "John's Run" is a pun on Union commander

David Y. Johns, who allegedly abandoned his troops during the fight. He resigned from service on November 11, 1861 (United States Adjutant-General's Office, *Official Army Register of the Volunteer Force of the United States Army*, 1,244).

210. *Cincinnati Daily Press*, "From Camp Enyart."

211. *Richmond Dispatch*, September 25, 1861.

212. National Park Service, "Civil War Soldiers and Sailors"; *Cincinnati Daily Press*, "Battle of John's Run."

213. *Richmond Dispatch*, September 25, 1861.

214. *Nashville Union and American*, "From Wise's Legion."

215. *Confederate Veteran*, "James H. Loughborough."

216. *Richmond Dispatch*, September 25, 1861.

217. *OR*, Series 2, 2:1,450.

218. *Richmond Times Dispatch*, September 25, 1861.

219. *Nashville Union and American*, "From Wise's Legion."

220. National Park Service, "Civil War Soldiers and Sailors."

221. Hale, "September 19, 1861."

222. *Cincinnati Daily Press*, "Battle of John's Run." The same newspaper printed an updated casualty list on September 30, 1861, which differed somewhat: "WOUNDED AND MISSING OF COMPANY D. Wounded—Lieutenant Morris, shot in the arm. Missing—Second Lieutenant James Farran; Sergeant Robert Healey; Corporal D.S. Dick; Privates Gordon Calvert, Michael Fitzgerrol, David Griffiths, James H. Gray, Fred Hillman, John Heinbach, Charles Kestenboitz, George W. Loyd, Jacob Leitt, Morris Mulaly, Samuel McElroy, Michael McDonald, John C. O'Brien, William Perkins, Jacob Schatzman, John Shokey, Martin Geager, David Young, Charles Hunt, supposed to be killed. WOUNDED AND MISSING OF COMPANY I. Dead—Sergeants A.R. Potter and J.M. Robinson; Private Fred Weber. Wounded—Privates Fred Artz, John Hasper and Morris Quinlin. Prisoners—Captain Thos. Cox; Sergeant J.G. Larrence; Corporals Edward Haines, C.C.H. Tittle and Martin Millipan; privates John Boltz, Wm. Conklin, Martin Good, Terry Kingsbury, Alonzo Railing, Charles Rupp, Fred Roseweyer, Thomas Vanfleet, and Israel Young." ("From Camp Enyart—List of the Killed, Wounded and Missing of Companies D and I of the First Kentucky Regiment," *Cincinnati Daily Press*, September 30, 1861).

223. *Cincinnati Daily Press*, "Battle of John's Run."

224. *OR*, 5:870.

225. *Richmond Examiner*, September 25, 1861.

226. Tyrrell, "Libby Prisoners," 561–67.

227. *Cincinnati Daily Press*, "Battle of John's Run."

228. Hewett, *Supplement to the Official Records*, Part 1, Vol. 1, Issue 1, 377.

229. *Richmond Dispatch*, September 25, 1861.

230. Hewett, *Supplement to the Official Records*, Part 1, Vol. 1, Issue 1, 377–78.

231. *Richmond Times Dispatch*, October 15, 1861.

232. Hewett, *Supplement to the Official Records*, Part 1, Vol. 1, Issue 1, 378.

233. Hale, "September 19, 1861."

234. Driver, *10th Virginia Cavalry*, 12.

235. *Kith and Kin of Boone County* XVIII, no. 3; *Kith and Kin of Boone County* XX, no. 1; National Park Service, "Civil War Soldiers and Sailors."

236. Henning and Rummel, *Toney Family History*, 305.

237. *Richmond Times Dispatch*, October 15, 1861; Ibid., "The Affair at Toney's," November 6, 1861.

CHAPTER 4

238. Hash and LaBelle, "Rockcastle Missionary Baptist Church."

239. *OR*, 2:1450.

240. Hager, *Boone County, West Virginia History*; Turner, "Floyd Cooke—An Early Settler on the Mountain."

241. *Staunton Spectator*, "The Mounted Rangers in the West," October 8, 1861.

242. *OR*, Series 2, Vol. 2, Part 1, 1451.

243. Ibid., Vol. 51, Part 2, 273.

244. White, *History of Cook Mountain*.

245. Richardson, *Raleigh County*.

246. *Richmond Times Dispatch*, "Caskie's Rangers in the West," August 8, 1861.

247. *OR*, Series 2, Vol. 2, Part 1, 1451, 1461–62. This fortification was labeled "formidable" in the *OR*, but the exact location is no longer known. While there are several claims to its location, references to Walnut Gap, Skin Fork and the settlement of Pond Fork suggest it was situated within that triangle, possibly overlooking present-day Burnt Camp Branch Road.

248. *OR*, Series 2, Vol. 2, Part 1, 1440. "Captain Pate [reported] that he had arrested a Captain or Lieutenant Miller." The company of volunteers that Miller was raising for Federal service was Company B, Eighth (West) Virginia Infantry, which included many Bald Knob area recruits.

249. 187th West Virginia Militia, Capt. Jos. H. Barker Co., Roll dated June 1, 1863.

250. Turner, "Floyd Cooke."

251. Jeffrey, *Richmond Prisons*, 23.

252. Haga, "Civil War Journal of William Sewell Dunbar."

CHAPTER 5

253. *OR*, Vol. 5, Part 1, 900–02.

254. *Raleigh Register*, May 25, 1959.

255. The *New York Times*, October 4, 1861, and *Harper's Weekly*, October 19, 1861, state that a company of the Fifth (West) Virginia Infantry Regiment also participated in the Kanawha Gap expedition, but to this date, no other supporting sources have been found.

256. *Daily Alta California*, "The Hardest March of the Campaign," November 1, 1861. The author of the report was probably Captain Andrew Hogan, Company J, First Kentucky Infantry Regiment.

257. Ibid.

258. Ibid.

259. *Cincinnati Gazette*, "Camp Enyart, October 1, 1861," October 2, 1861.

260. Journey Up Coal River, "History of Coal River Part 1."

261. *Bucyrus Journal*, October 18, 1861.

262. Sparks, "100th Anniversary Celebration." Sparks (OT) indicates that the Confederate cavalry was from Tazewell, Virginia, and was possibly Company H, Eighth Virginia Cavalry, originally known as the Tazewell Troopers or McDonald's company and composed of men from both Mercer and Tazewell Counties. The company was formed by Captain John C. McDonald on July 25, 1861. The Twenty-eighth Militia Brigade of Tazewell, Buchanan and McDowell Counties was at Raleigh Court House on September 23, 1861, when it received orders from Floyd to send two hundred men through Wyoming to Logan County to gather news on the enemy (*Raleigh Register*, "Raleigh County Split During Civil War," June 19, 1863). *The Papers of Jefferson Davis, 1862* (8:122) indicates that Colonel Davis was commanding a Virginia cavalry battalion at Chapmanville.

263. Moore, *Rebellion Record*, 149.

264. *Bucyrus Journal*, October 18, 1861.

265. *Compiled Records*, Virginia reel, 299.

266. Williams, "A Brief History."

267. *Cincinnati Commercial*, October 8, 1861.

268. Ibid.

269. Williams, "A Brief History."

270. *Bucyrus Journal*, October 18, 1861.

271. Williams, "A Brief History."

272. Ibid.

273. *Staunton Spectator*, "Fight in Logan County," October 22, 1861.

274. *Bucyrus Journal*, October 18, 1861.

275. *Cincinnati Commercial*, October 8, 1861. The 129th Regiment's Captain Baisden reported 225 militia at Chapmanville (*Compiled Records*, Virginia reel, 299).

276. Moore, *Rebellion Record*, 177.
277. *Cincinnati Commercial*, October 8, 1861.
278. Pollard, *Southern History of the War*, 176.
279. *Bucyrus Journal*, October 18, 1861.
280. *American Annual Cyclopedia*, 741.
281. *New York Times*, "Fighting in the Kanawha," October 4, 1861.
282. *Bucyrus Journal*, October 18, 1861. It is supposed that the Confederate surgeon was Vandelinde of the Boone militia. Stough's report corroborates local tradition that Vandelinde provided medical care to both sides during the war and was skilled in amputation.
283. *Cincinnati Commercial*, October 8, 1861.
284. *Bucyrus Journal*, October 18, 1861.
285. *New York Times*, "Fighting in the Kanawha," October 4, 1861.
286. *National Republican*, October 7, 1861.

CHAPTER 6

287. There were also noncombat losses omitted from compilations of the casualties. These include civilian deaths due to famine and disease that autumn and winter. In addition, the burnings of Boone Court House, Bloomingrose and Bald Knob resulted in making hundreds of people homeless, further contributing to and exacerbating the human misery.
288. *New York Times*, "The Fight at Boone Court-House," September 8, 1861.
289. *OR*, Vol. 5, Part 1, 501–03.
290. Snell, *West Virginia and the Civil War*, 55.
291. McCoy, *Last Grace*, 226.
292. *OR*, Vol. 51, Part 1, 513–14.
293. Debates and Proceedings of the First Constitutional Convention of West Virginia, December 7, 1861, by Robert Hager of Boone County. Slavery was an issue that hung over the convention. On November 30, 1861, it was Hager who called for a free state and proposed gradual emancipation of slavery throughout the new state.
294. Haga, "Civil War Journal of William Sewell Dunbar."
295. Ibid.
296. Ibid. The location of this affair is determined by the reference to "Stover's place," which is established in Stover, "Stover Descendants."
297. *Raleigh Register*, May 25, 1959.
298. Few today with Civil War–era ties to the area do not have stories passed down—via correspondence, letters, diaries and oral tradition—of the bloody, indelible stain and rifts the suffering and sacrifice caused by the war left on the Coal River Valley.

299. Johnston, *History of the Middle New River Settlements*, 200–01.

300. Summers, *Mountain State*, 123–24.

301. U.S. Census Bureau, "U.S. Census Population Schedule, 1870."

302. *OR*, 5:501–03.

303. Pettry, "The Killing of Andrew Gunnoe."

304. Bowman, *Reference Book of Wyoming County History*, 126. James Anderson Gunnoe (1841–1924), a son of Andrew Gunnoe, was a sergeant in the Forty-fifth Virginia Infantry Battalion. After the war, he was tried and convicted in 1866 of second-degree murder in the death of Whitt and served two years in the West Virginia State Penitentiary before he was pardoned. He was the only man ever sent to prison for a crime that was committed as part of the Civil War (Blankenship, "Heinous Deed of 1863 Recalled," *Wyoming County Report*, April, 22, 2013).

305. OT, Price.

306. "The Killing of Andrew Gunnoe," in James R. Pettry, *Kith and Kin of Boone County, West Virginia*, Vol. XIV.

307. *Richmond Times Dispatch*, April 29, 1862.

308. Hewett, *Supplement to the Official Records*, Part 2, Volume 74, Issue 86, 230.

309. Sedinger, "War-Time Reminiscences of James D. Sedinger," 55–78.

310. *OR*, 21:1104–07.

311. Saunier, *History of the Forty-seventh Regiment*.

312. *OR*, 21:22–23.

313. Brinkerhoff, *History of the 30th Regiment*, 51–53.

314. Ibid., 25:44.

315. Sutton, *History of the Second Regiment*.

316. *OR*, Vol. 27, Part 2, 792–93.

317. Maginnis, "Confederate-Union Skirmishes."

318. Johnston, *History of the Middle New River Settlements*, 267–68.

319. *OR*, 29:493–94.

320. Riffe, "Early Settlers of Raleigh County, West Virginia."

321. Maginnis, "Confederate-Union Skirmishes." Chapman is cited as a major. See also *Hardesty's Historical and Geographical Encyclopedia*.

322. Captain William Summer, letter from Kanawha County, West Virginia, November 2, 1864, to Governor Boreman, http://www.wvculture.org/history/wvmemory/militia/kanawha/kanawha1.html.

323. In June 2011, the West Virginia legislature designated State Route 26 from Van to Twilight in Boone County as a Civil War Veterans Memorial Highway for Private William Chapman "Chap" Cook, one of Floyd Cooke's sons, who served in the Seventh West Virginia Cavalry.

Bibliography

Unpublished Primary Sources

Boone County Genealogical Society, Madison, West Virginia. http://www.rootsweb.ancestry.com/~wvbcgs/. Genealogical sources.

Boone-Madison Public Library, Madison, West Virginia. Genealogical sources.

George Tyler Moore Center for the Study of the Civil War, Shepherd University, Shepherdstown, West Virginia. Compiled military service records (Virginia, West Virginia).

John W. Morrow Library, Marshall University, Huntington, West Virginia. Special Civil War Historical Collection.

Library of Virginia, Richmond, Virginia. Database of Virginia Military Dead. http://www.lva.virginia.gov/public/guides/vmd/.

National Archives and Records Administration, Washington, D.C. Compiled Military Service Records (Kentucky, Ohio, Virginia, West Virginia). Microfilm reels.

———. *Compiled Records Showing Service of Military Units in Confederate Organizations*. Washington, D.C.: National Archives and Record Service, 1971.

——— *Compiled Records Showing Service of Military Units in Volunteer Union Organizations*. Washington, D.C.: National Archives and Record Service, 1965.

National Archives and Records Service. Civil War Letters, Orders and Records of Brig. General Henry A. Wise and the Wise Brigade.

———. *Military Operations of the Civil War: A Guide-Index to the Official Records of the Union and Confederate Armies, 1861–1865*. Washington, D.C.: U.S. Government Printing Office, 1968.

National Park Service. Civil War Soldiers and Sailors System. http://www. itd.nps.gov/cwss/index.html.

United States Army Military History Institute, Carlisle Barracks, Pennsylvania. Civil War Collection.

West Virginia Division of Culture and History, Charleston, West Virginia. "Child of the Rebellion." http://www.wvculture.org/history/ sesquicentennial/18610930.html.

———. Debates and Proceedings of the First Constitutional Convention of West Virginia. http://www.wvculture.org/history/statehood/cc120461.html.

———. Online Militia Records. http://www.wvculture.org/history/ wvsamenu.html.

West Virginia University Library, West Virginia University, Morgantown, West Virginia. West Virginia and Regional History Collection and Special Collections.

PUBLISHED PRIMARY SOURCES

Letters, Diaries and Journals

C. Stratton. Letter from Peytona, Boone County, Virginia, June 20, 1862. http://www.pwcvirginia.com/documents/PeytonaBooneCountyletter.pdf.

Haga, Pauline. "Civil War Journal of William Sewell Dunbar." *Historical Footprints*. Vol. 1. http://www.wvgenweb.org/raleigh/Footprints/index.htm.

Hale, Francis G. "September 19, 1861." Civil War Diaries of Francis G. Hale [manuscript], 1861–1864, Accession #13405, Special Collections, University of Virginia Library, Charlottesville, Virginia.

Summer, Captain William. Letter from Kanawha County, West Virginia, November 2, 1864, to Governor Boreman. http://www.wvculture.org/ history/wvmemory/militia/kanawha/kanawha1.html.

Government Documents

Adjutant General, State of West Virginia. *Annual Report for the Year Ended December 31, 1865*. Wheeling, WV: John Frew, printer, 1866.

Ambler, Charles Henry. *Debates and Proceedings of the First Constitutional Convention of West Virginia, 1861–1863*. Huntington, WV: Gentry Brothers, 1941.

Kentucky Adjutant General's Office. *Report of the Adjutant General of the State of Kentucky*, Vol. 1, 1861–1866. Frankfort: Kentucky Yeoman Office, Public Printer, 1866.

Rockbridge County Court. "The Rockbridge Rangers." Court Minutes, 1898–1903. Rockbridge County Court, Rockbridge County, Virginia. http://files.usgwarchives.net/va/rockbridge/courts/minutes-1898-1903.txt.

United States Adjutant-General's Office. *Official Army Register of the Volunteer Force of the United States Army*. Washington, D.C.: U.S. Government Printing Office, 1865.

United States War Department. *The War of the Rebellion: A Compilation of the Official Records of the Union and Confederate Armies*. Washington, D.C.: U.S. Government Printing Office, 1880–1901.

U.S. Army Military History Institute. *Unit Bibliography*. Carlisle Barracks, PA: U.S. Army Military History Institute, 1995.

U.S. Census Bureau. "U.S. Census Population Schedule, 1850." Boone County, Virginia, United States Census Office. 7th Census. Digital images of originals housed at the National Archives, Washington, D.C.

———. "U.S. Census Population Schedule, 1860." Boone County, Virginia, United States Census Office. 8th Census. Digital images of originals housed at the National Archives, Washington, D.C.

———. "U.S. Census Population Schedule, 1870." Boone County, West Virginia, United States Census Office. 9th Census. Digital images of originals housed at the National Archives, Washington, D.C.

Virginia Board of Public Works. *Annual Report of the Board of Public Works to the General Assembly of Virginia, with the Accompanying Documents*. Vol. 36. Richmond: Virginia Board of Public Works, 1851.

Memoirs and Reminiscences

Cox, Jacob D. *Military Reminiscences of the Civil War*. New York: Scribner, 1900.

Hash, Lee, and Patricia LaBelle. "The Rockcastle Missionary Baptist Church: The First 100 Years." Joel Hager's Southern West Virginia Research. http://wc.rootsweb.ancestry.com/cgi-bin/igm.cgi?op=GET&db=hagerj&id=I216735.

Hufford, Mary. Interview with Howard Miller. American Folklife Center, Library of Congress. Washington, D.C. http://auroralights.org/map_project/theme.php?theme=coal_river_101&article=primary.

McClellan, George B. *McClellan's Own Story: The War for the Union*. New York: Charles L. Webster, 1887.

———. *Report of Maj.-Gen. George B. McClellan, Aug. 4, 1863—Army of the Potomac—with an Account of the Campaign in Western Virginia*. New York: Sheldon and Company, 1864. Reprint, Proctorville, OH: Mark S. Phillips Publishing, 2008.

Peyton, John Lewis. *Memoir of William Madison Peyton.* London: John Wilson, 1873.

Williams, John. "A Brief History of My Army Life as I Saw It." http://www.geocaching.com/seek/cache_details.aspx?guid=a62cee70-4fef-4ac2-86b5-b405cb8e430e.

Oral Tradition

Tet V. Chumley (1918–2003)
Ruth V. Miller (1917–)
Denver D. Roush (1910–1981)

Newspapers and Magazines

American and Commercial Advertiser (Baltimore). "Fight Between Union Men and Secessionists at Boone Court House—The Secessionists Defeated." September 3, 1861.

Blankenship, Paul Ray. "Heinous Deed of 1863 Recalled." *Wyoming County Report*, April, 22, 2013.

Bucyrus Journal (Ohio). October 18, 1861.

Charleston Daily Mail (Charleston, WV). May 19, 1929.

Charleston Gazette (Charleston, WV). July 18, 1948.

Cincinnati Commercial. October 8, 1861.

Cincinnati Daily Press. "Battle of John's Run: Another Fight in Western Virginia-Rebels Victorious—Two Companies of the First Kentucky Regiment Badly Cut Up—Hard Fighting." September 19, 1861.

———. "From Camp Enyart—List of the Killed, Wounded and Missing of Companies D and I of the First Kentucky Regiment." September 30, 1861.

———. September 13, 1861.

Cincinnati Gazette. "Camp Enyart, October 1, 1861." October 2, 1861.

———. "The Fight at Boone Court-House." September 5, 1861.

Civilian and Gazette Weekly (Galveston, TX). October 15, 1861.

Cleveland Morning Leader. "Late from the Kanawha—The Fight at Boone." September 6, 1861.

Coal Valley News (Madison, WV). "The History of Boone County." February 29, 1990.

Cunningham, Sumner Archibald, and Edith D. Pope, eds. *Confederate Veteran* magazine, 40 volumes. Nashville: S. A. Cunningham, 1893–1932.

Currey, Bill. "The Coal River," *West Virginia Magazine* (June 2005): 8-11.

Daily Alta California. "The Hardest March of the Campaign." November 1, 1861.

Daily Nashville Patriot. "Boon Courthouse, Va. Burnt by Federal Scoundrels." September 24, 1861.

Dreasy, Timothy. "The 26th Ohio." *National Tribune*, December 20, 1906.

Evening Star. "The Battle of Kanawha Gap." October 11, 1861.

Frank Leslie's Illustrated Newspaper. November 8, 1862.

Fremont Journal (Fremont, Ohio). "The Fight at Boone Court House." September 20, 1861.

Gallipolis Journal. "Details of the Boone Court House Fight." September 12, 1861.

———. September 5, 1861.

Hoeft, Michael. "A Colorful History Surrounds Southern W.Va.'s Coal River," *West Virginia Magazine* (May 1995): 22–26.

Long, Leander. "Army Correspondence [September 5, 1861]." *Urbana Citizen and Gazette*, September 19, 1861.

Louisville Courier. September 6, 1861.

Maginnis, William H. "Confederate-Union Skirmishes Mark Earliest History of Lincoln County." *Charleston Gazette*, July 4, 1948.

National Republican. October 7, 1861.

New York Herald. December 14, 1862.

New York Sun. "Another Victory in Western Virginia." September 7, 1861.

New York Times. "Another Victory of the National Troops." September 3, 1861.

———. "The Fight at Boone Court-House." September 8, 1861.

———. "Fighting in the Kanawha; Rebels Routed at Chapmanville." October 4, 1861.

———. July 23, 1861.

Raleigh Register. "Raleigh County Split During Civil War, Beckley Was Key Point of Contention." June 19, 1963.

Richmond Examiner. September 25, 1861.

Richmond Times Dispatch. "The Affair at Toney's." November 6, 1861.

———. May 24, 1861.

———. August 8, 1861.

———. September 9, 1861.

———. September 11, 1861.

———. September 25, 1861.

———. October 7, 1861.

———. October 15, 1861.

———. April 29, 1862.

Riffe, W.A. "Early Settlers of Raleigh County, West Virginia." *Beckley Post-Herald*, August 26, 1950.

Rolla Express (Phelps County, MO). September 9, 1861.

Spirit of Democracy (Woodfield, Ohio). "Fight at Boone Court House." September 11, 1861.

Staunton Spectator. "The Mounted Rangers in the West." October 8, 1861.

Stutler, Boyd B. "Boone and Logan Court Houses Burned." *Raleigh Register,* May 25, 1959.

Tazewell (VA) Democrat. September 14, 1861.

Tyrrell, Henry. "Libby Prisoners. A Thanksgiving Episode of '61." *The American Magazine,* Vol. 38. New York: Frank Leslie's, 1894.

Virginia Gazetteer. 1835–57 editions.

Wheeling Intelligencer. "The First West Virginia Legislature. House of Delegates. Sketches Personal, Political and Biographical. Robert Hager, from Boone." September 9, 1863.

———. January 1–December 31, 1863.

SECONDARY SOURCES

Books

The American Annual Cyclopedia and Register of Important Events of the Year 1861. New York: Appleton, 1864.

Andre, Richard, Stan Cohen, and Bill Wintz. *Bullets and Steel: The Fight for the Great Kanawha Valley, 1861–1865.* Charleston, WV: Pictorial Histories Publishing Co., 1995.

Atkinson, George Wesley, and Alvaro Franklin Gibbens. *Prominent Men of West Virginia: Biographical Sketches, the Growth and Advancement of the State, a Compendium of Returns of Every Election, a Record of Every State Officer.* Wheeling, WV: W.L. Callin, 1890.

Boatner, Mark M. *The Civil War Dictionary.* New York: Vintage Press, 1991.

Boone County Genealogical Society. *Kith and Kin of Boone County, West Virginia.* Madison, WV: Boone County Genealogical Society, 1978–83.

Bowman, Mary Keller. *Reference Book of Wyoming County History.* Privately published, 1965.

Brinkerhoff, Henry R. *History of the 30th Regiment, Ohio Volunteer Infantry from Its Organization to the Fall of Vicksburg, Miss.* Columbus, OH: J.W. Osgood, printer, 1863.

Callahan, James Morton. *History of West Virginia, Old and New, in One Volume, and West Virginia Biography, in Two Additional Volumes.* Chicago: American Historical Society, 1923.

Carr, Michael W. "Timothy H. Deasy." In *A History of Catholicity in Northern Ohio and the Diocese of Cleveland from 1749 to December 31, 1900.* Cleveland, OH: J.B. Savage Press, 1903.

Casto, Mitch. *Boone County, West Virginia History: A Time Line and Source Book.* Madison, WV: Boone-Madison Public Library, 1994.

Catton, Bruce. *The Coming Fury.* New York: Doubleday, 1961.

———. *Terrible Swift Sword.* New York: Doubleday, 1963.

Cohen, Stan. *The Civil War in West Virginia: A Pictorial History.* Charleston, WV: Pictorial Histories Publishing Co., 1976.

———. *A Pictorial Guide to West Virginia Civil War Sites and Related Information.* Charleston, WV: Quarrier Press, 1990.

Cole, Scott. *34th Battalion Virginia Cavalry.* Lynchburg: Virginia Regimental Histories, 1993.

Commager, Henry Steele, ed. *The Blue and the Gray.* 2 vols. Indianapolis, IN: Bobbs-Merrill, 1950.

Cooper, Charles R. *Chronological and Alphabetical Record of the Engagements of the Great Civil War with the Casualties on Both Sides.* Milwaukee, WI: Caxton, 1904.

Creasey, Edward S. *Fifteen Decisive Battles of the World from Marathon to Waterloo.* New York: Da Capo, 1994.

Cushing, Marshall Henry. *Story of Our Post Office: The Greatest Government Department in All Its Phases.* Boston: A.M. Thayer & Company, 1893.

Davis, Carl L. *Arming the Union: Small Arms in the Civil War.* Port Washington, NY: Kennikat Press, 1973.

Davis, Jefferson. *The Papers of Jefferson Davis, 1862.* Edited by Mary Seaton Dix and Haskell M. Monroe. Baton Rouge: Louisiana State University Press, 1995.

Dean, Bill. *Coal, Steamboats, Timber and Trains: The Industrial History of St. Albans, West Virginia, and the Coal River Valley, 1850–1925.* Charleston, WV: Pictorial Histories Publishing, 2008.

Dickinson, Jack L. *8th Virginia Cavalry.* Lynchburg, VA: H.E. Howard, 1986.

———. *16th Virginia Cavalry.* Lynchburg: Virginia Regimental Histories, 1989.

———. *Tattered Uniforms and Bright Bayonets: West Virginia's Confederate Soldiers.* Huntington WV: Marshall University Library Association, 1995.

Dilts, Bryan L. *1890 West Virginia Census Index of Civil War Veterans or Their Widows.* Salt Lake City, UT: Index Publishing, 1986.

Dornbusch, Charles E. *Military Bibliography of the Civil War.* 3 vols. New York: New York Public Library, 1961–72.

Dowdy, Clifford, ed. *The Wartime Papers of R.E. Lee.* Boston: Little, Brown and Company, 1961.

Driver, Robert J. *10th Virginia Cavalry.* Lynchburg, VA: H.E. Howard, 1992.

Dyer, Frederick H. *A Compendium of the War of the Rebellion Compiled and Arranged from Official Records of the Federal and Confederate Armies Reports of the Adjutant Generals of the Several States, the Army Registers and Other Reliable Documents and Sources.* 3 vols. Dayton, OH: Morningside Bookshop, 1978 [1908].

Evans, Clement A., ed. *Confederate Military History: Maryland and West Virginia.* 13 volumes. Atlanta: Confederate Publishing Company, 1899.

Fishel, Edwin C. *The Secret War for the Union: The Untold Story of Military Intelligence in the Civil War.* Boston: Houghton Mifflin Company, 1996.

Fluharty, Linda C. *Civil War—West Virginia—Union Lives Lost.* Baton Rouge, LA: self-published, 2004.

Foote, Shelby. *The Civil War: A Narrative.* 3 vols. New York: Random House, 1958–74.

Fox, William F. *Regimental Losses in the American Civil War, 1861–1865: A Treatise on the Extent and Nature of the Mortuary Losses in the Union Regiments, with Full and Exhaustive Statistics Compiled from the Official Records on File in the State Military Bureaus and at Washington.* Albany, NY: Albany Publishing Company, 1889.

Freeman, Douglas Southall, ed. *Lee's Dispatches: Unpublished Letters of General Robert E. Lee, C.S.A., to Jefferson Davis and the War Department of the Confederate States of America, 1862–65.* New York: G.P. Putnam's Sons, 1957.

———. *Lee's Lieutenants: A Study in Command.* 3 vols. New York: Charles Scribner's Sons, 1942–44.

———. *R.E. Lee.* 4 vols. New York: Charles Scribner's Sons, 1934–35.

Goodspeed, Arthur G. *History of the Goodspeed Family.* Madison: University of Wisconsin-Madison, 1907.

Hager, Ira. *Blue and Grey Battlefields.* Parsons, WV: McClain Printing, 1978.

Hager, Janet B. *Boone County, West Virginia History.* Madison, WV: Boone County Genealogical Society, 1990.

Hale, John P. *History of the Great Kanawha Valley.* 2 vols. Madison, WI: Brant, Fuller & Co., 1891.

Hardesty's Historical and Geographical Encyclopedia: Special History of the Virginias, Maps and Histories of Wayne, Lincoln and Cabell Counties, West Virginia. Chicago: H.H. Hardesty, 1884.

Hatfield, Philip. *The Other Feud: William Anderson "Devil Anse" Hatfield in the Civil War.* N.p.: CreateSpace, 2010.

Henderson, G.F.R. *Stonewall Jackson and the American Civil War.* New York: Longmans, Green and Co., 1898.

Henning, Elma, and Merle Rummel. *The Toney Family History.* Louisville, KY: Gateway Press, 1979.

Hewett, Janet B. *The Roster of Union Soldiers, 1861–1865.* Vol. 4. Wilmington, NC: Broadfoot Publishing, 1999.

———. *Supplement to the Official Records of the Union and Confederate Armies* (Part 2, Volume 74, Issue 86). Wilmington, NC: Broadfoot Publishing Company, 1998.

———. *Supplement to the Official Records of the Union and Confederate Armies* (Part 2, Volume 51, Issue 63). Wilmington, NC: Broadfoot Publishing Company, 1997.

———. *Supplement to the Official Records of the Union and Confederate Armies* (Part 1, Volume 1, Issue 1). Wilmington, NC: Broadfoot Publishing Company, 1994.

Hill, Jeffrey A. *The 26th Ohio Veteran Volunteer Infantry: The Groundhog Regiment.* N.p.: Authorhouse, 2010.

Jeffrey, William H. *Richmond Prisons, 1861–1862.* St. Johnsbury, VT: Republican Press, 1893.

Johnson, R.V., and C.C. Buel, eds. *Battles and Leaders of the Civil War.* 3 vols. New York: The Century Company, 1887–88.

Johnston, David E. *A History of the Middle New River Settlements and Contiguous Territory.* Huntington, WV: Standard Printing and Publishing Co., 1906.

Keegan, John. *A History of Warfare.* New York: Alfred A. Knopf, 1993.

Keifer, Joseph Warren. *Civil War Regiments from Ohio.* Madison, WI: Federal Publishing Company, 1908.

Kelly, Welden. *A Historic Sketch: Lest We Forget Company E, 26th Ohio Infantry in the War for the Union, 1861–1865.* Osborn, MO, 1909.

Krebs, C.E., D.D. Teets Jr. and I.C. White. *West Virginia Geological Survey: Boone County.* Wheeling, WV: Wheeling News Litho. Co., 1915.

Lang, Theodore F. *Loyal West Virginia from 1861 to 1865.* Baltimore, MD: Deutsch Publishing Co., 1895.

Lewis, Billie Redding. *Pioneers of the Virginias.* Lake Wales, FL: privately published, 1988.

Linger, James Carter. *Confederate Military Units of West Virginia.* Tulsa, OK: privately published, 2002.

Livermore, Thomas L. *Numbers and Losses in the Civil War in America, 1861–65.* Bloomington: Indiana University Press, 1957.

Lonn, Ella. *Desertion During the Civil War.* New York: The Century Company, 1928.

Lowry, Terry. *The Battle of Scary Creek: Military Operations in the Kanawha Valley, April–July 1861.* Charleston, WV: Pictorial Histories Publishing Company, 1998.

———. *Last Sleep: Battle Of Droop Mountain.* Charleston, WV: Pictorial Histories Publishing Company, 1996.

———. *22nd Virginia Infantry.* Lynchburg, VA: H.E. Howard, 1988.

Lowry, Terry, and Stan Cohen. *Images of the Civil War in West Virginia.* Charleston, WV: Pictorial Histories Publishing Company, 2000.

McCoy, Sid. *The Last Grace.* N.p.: iUniverse, 2012.

McKinney, Tim. *The Civil War in Fayette County, West Virginia.* Charleston, WV: Pictorial Histories Publishing Company, 1988.

———. *Robert E. Lee and the 35th Star.* Charleston, WV: Pictorial Histories Publishing Company, 1993.

———. *West Virginia Civil War Almanac.* Vol. 1. Charleston, WV: Pictorial Histories Publishing Company, 1998.

———. *West Virginia Civil War Almanac.* Vol. 2. Charleston, WV: Quarrier Press, 2000.

McManus, Howard R. *The Battle of Cloyd's Mountain: The Virginia and Tennessee Railroad Raid, April 29–May 19, 1864.* Lynchburg, VA: H.E. Howard, 1989.

McPherson, James M. *Battle Cry of Freedom: The Civil War Era.* New York: Oxford University Press, 1988.

Miller, Everett W. *Genealogy of Jacob Miller and His Descendants.* Huntington, WV: Cook, 1952.

Miller, Francis T. *Photographic History of the Civil War: The Navies.* New York: Review of Reviews, 1911.

Millett, Allan R., and Peter Maslowski. *For the Common Defense: A Military History of the United States of America.* New York: Free Press, 1984.

Moore, Frank. *The Rebellion Record: A Diary of American Events.* New York: D. Van Nostrand, 1869.

Mosocco, Ronald. *The Chronological Tracking of the American Civil War Per the Official Records of the War of the Rebellion.* Williamsburg, VA: James River Publications, 1994.

Newell, Clayton. *Lee vs. McClellan: The First Campaign.* Washington, D.C.: Gateway, 1996.

Newman, Harry Wright. *The Smoots of Maryland and Virginia.* Washington, D.C.: privately published, 1936; later edition edited and published by Frederick K. Smoot and the Smoot Family Association, 2001.

Noe, Kenneth W. *The Civil War in Appalachia.* Knoxville: University of Tennessee Press, 1997.

Official Roster of Soldiers of the State of Ohio in the War of the Rebellion. 12 vols. Akron, OH: Werner Company, 1886–95.

Olafson, Sigfus. "The Smoot Family of Boone County, West Virginia." *Kith and Kin of Boone County, West Virginia.* Vol. 3. Madison, WV: Boone County Genealogical Society, 1978.

Osborne, Randall, and Jeffrey C. Weaver. *The Virginia State Rangers and State Line.* Lynchburg: Virginia Regimental Histories, 1994.

Phillips, David L. *Civil War Stories: Civil War in West Virginia.* Leesburg, VA: Gauley Mount Press, 1991.

———. *War Diaries: The 1861 Kanawha Valley Campaign.* Leesburg, VA: Gauley Mount Press, 1990.

Phisterer, Frederick. *Statistical Record of the Armies of the United States.* New York: Charles Scribner's Sons, 1883.

Pinkerton, Allan. *The Spy of the Rebellion; Being a True History of the Spy System of the United States Army During the War of the Rebellion.* New York: G.W. Carleton & Co., 1883.

Pollard, E.A. *Southern History of the War: First Year of the War.* Richmond, VA: West and Johnson, 1862.

Rees, E., and C.W. Rees. *Condensed Chronological History of the Great Rebellion in the United States.* San Francisco: Defferbach, 1867.

Reid, Whitelaw. *Ohio in the War: Her Statesmen, Her Generals and Soldiers*. Cincinnati, OH: Moore, Wilstach & Baldwin, 1868.

Richardson, H.A. *Raleigh County, West Virginia, in the Civil War*. Morgantown: West Virginia University Press, 1943.

Saunier, Joseph A. *A History of the Forty-Seventh Regiment, Ohio Veteran Volunteer Infantry*. Salem, OH: Lyle Printing Company, 1903.

Scott, J.L.. *60th Virginia Infantry*. Lynchburg, VA: H.E. Howard, 1997.

———. *36th Virginia Infantry*. Lynchburg, VA: H.E. Howard, 1987.

Shanks, Henry T. *The Secession Movement in Virginia, 1857–1861*. Richmond, VA: Garrett and Massie, 1934.

Sifakis, Stewart. "Compendium of the Confederate Armies: Virginia." *Facts on File*, 1992.

Smith, Edward C. *The Borderland in the Civil War*. Freeport, NY: Books for Libraries Press, 1927.

Snell, Mark A. *West Virginia and the Civil War: Mountaineers Are Always Free*. Charleston, SC: The History Press, 2011.

Southern History of the War. Official Reports of Battles, as Published by Order of the Confederate Congress at Richmond. (Published in two parts). New York: Charles B. Richardson, 1863.

Southern Historical Society, comp. *Southern Historical Society Papers*. 52 vols. Richmond: Virginia Historical Society, 1876–59.

Spaulding, Melburn C., comp. *Records of Official Correspondence of the Federal and Confederate Armies in the Kanawha River Valley, 1861–1864*. Tantallon, MD, 1976.

Speed, Thomas, et al. *The Union Regiments of Kentucky*. Louisville, KY: Union Soldiers and Sailors Monument Association, 1897.

Strickler, Theodore D. *When and Where We Met Each Other: On Shore and Afloat: Battles, Engagements, Actions, Skirmishes, and Expeditions During the Civil War, 1861–1865*. Washington, D.C.: National Tribune, circa 1899.

Stutler, Boyd B. *The Campaign in West Virginia, 1861*. Columbus: Ohio Historical Society, 1961.

———. *West Virginia in the Civil War*. N.p.: West Virginia Education Foundation, 1966.

Summers, George. *The Mountain State: A Description of the Natural Resources of West Virginia*. Charleston, WV: Donnally, 1893.

Sutherland, Daniel E. *Guerillas, Unionists, and Violence on the Confederate Home Front*. Fayetteville: University of Arkansas Press, 1999.

Sutton, Joseph J. *History of the Second Regiment, West Virginia Cavalry Volunteers During the War of the Rebellion*. 1892. Reprint, Huntington, WV: Blue Acorn Press, 1992.

Turner, David A. *Genealogy of the Floyd Cooke Family of Boone County, West Virginia*. N.p.: privately published, 1980.

Turner, David A., and Ronald R. Turner. *Boone County, West Virginia Civil War Soldiers—The Turner Papers.* Vol. 2. Manassas, VA: Ronald Ray Turner, 2002.

Turner, Ronald R. *7th West Virginia Cavalry.* Manassas, VA: R.R. Turner, 1989.

Vandelinde, Bob L. *The Vandelinde Era, 1813–1996.* Emerald Isle, NC: B.L. Vandelinde, 1996.

Victor, Orville James. *The History, Civil, Political and Military, of the Southern Rebellion, from Its Incipient Stages to Its Close.* Vol. 2. New York: J.D. Torrey, 1861.

Walker, Gary C. *The War in Southwest Virginia, 1861–65.* Roanoke, VA: A&W Enterprise, 1985.

Wallace, Lee A., Jr. *A Guide to Virginia Military Organizations, 1861–1865.* Richmond, VA: Virginia Civil War Commission, 1964.

Warner, Ezra J. *Generals in Blue: Lives of the Union Commanders.* Baton Rouge: Louisiana State University Press, 1964.

———. *Generals in Gray: Lives of the Confederate Commanders.* Baton Rouge: Louisiana State University Press, 1959.

Weaver, Jeffrey C. *45th Battalion Virginia Infantry, Smith and Count's Battalions of Partisan Rangers.* Lynchburg, VA: H.E. Howard, 1994.

Weigley, Russell F. *The American Way of War: A History of United States Military Strategy and Policy.* New York: Macmillan, 1973.

———. *The History of the United States Army.* New York: Macmillan, 1967.

Welcher, Frank J. *The Union Army, 1861–1865: Organizations and Operations.* 2 vols. Bloomington: Indiana University Press, 1989, 1993.

White, Albert B. *First Biennial Message of Governor Albert B. White to the Legislature of West Virginia, Session of 1903.* Charleston, WV: Tribune Co., 1903.

Wiley, Bell I. *The Life of Billy Yank: The Common Soldier of the Union.* Baton Rouge: Louisiana State University Press, 1952.

———. *The Life of Johnny Reb: The Common Soldier of the Confederacy.* Baton Rouge: Louisiana State University Press, 1943.

Wise, Barton H. *Life of Henry A. Wise of Virginia, 1806–1876.* New York: MacMillan, 1899.

Wood, Jim. *Raleigh County, West Virginia.* Beckley, WV: BJW Printing and Office Supplies, 1994.

Wood, W.J. *Battles of the Revolutionary War, 1775–1781.* Boston: Da Capo, 2003.

Journals and Anthologies

Belohlavek, John M. "John B. Floyd and the West Virginia Campaign of 1861." *West Virginia History* 29 (July 1968): 283–91.

Curry, Richard O. "McClellan's Western Virginia Campaign of 1861." *Ohio History* 71, no. 2 (July 1962).

Forbes, Harold M. "John Peter Salling." *The West Virginia Encyclopedia*. http://www.wvencyclopedia.org/articles/167.

Hacker, J. David. "A Census-Based Count of the Civil War Dead." *Civil War History* 57, no. 4 (December 2011): 307–48.

Johnson, Mary E., and Joe Geiger Jr. "West Virginia's Militia and Home Guard in the Civil War." *West Virginia History* 58 (1999–2000): 68–167.

Klement, Frank. "General John B. Floyd and the West Virginia Campaign of 1861." *West Virginia History* 8 (April 1947): 319–33.

Richardson, Hila A. "Raleigh County, West Virginia in the Civil War." *West Virginia History* 10 (1949): 283–98.

Sedinger, James D. "War-Time Reminiscences of James D. Sedinger, Company E, 8th Virginia Cavalry (Border Rangers)." *West Virginia History* 51 (1992).

Weiss, Herbert K. "Combat Models and Historical Data: The U.S. Civil War." *Operations Research: The Journal of the Operations Research Society of America* 14 (September–October 1966): 759–90.

West Virginia Department of Archives and History. *West Virginia History* (1997): 56–58.

Manuscripts

Barloon, Mark C. "Combat Reconsidered: A Statistical Analysis of Small-Unit Actions During the American Civil War." Diss., University of North Texas, 2001.

Boehm, Robert B. "The Civil War in Western Virginia: The Decisive Campaigns of 1861." Diss., Ohio State University, 1957.

Branham, James. "Arbitrary Arrest in West Virginia, 1861–1865." Master's thesis, West Virginia University, 1959.

Guerci, Mark. "It Took a War: The End of Slavery in West Virginia." Thesis, College of William and Mary, 2011.

Jamieson, Perry D. "The Development of Civil War Tactics." Diss., Wayne State University, 1979.

Kucera, Peter G. "Brigadier General Henry A. Wise, C.S.A, and the Western Virginia Campaign of 1861." U.S. Army Command & General Staff College, 1980.

MacKenzie, Scott A. "The Civil War In Kanawha County, West Virginia, 1860–1865." Master's thesis, University of Calgary, 2007.

Moore, George E. "West Virginia and the Civil War." University of Chicago, 1921.

Short, Opha Masa. "General John B. Floyd in the Civil War." West Virginia University, 1947.

Stealley, John Edmund III. "The Salt Industry of the Great Kanawha Valley of Virginia: A Study in Ante-bellum Internal Commerce." West Virginia University, 1970.

Stover, George. "Stover Descendants." http://www.wvgenweb.org/raleigh/BOOK/StoverJohnGeorge.pdf.

Vargo, Emily. "The Little Coal River Improvement Project, West Virginia: An Initial Study of Sediment, Bacteria and Benthic Macroinvertebrates." Marshall University, 2011.

Internet and Digital Resources

Bullard, Leander S. "1890 Veterans Census, Crook District, Boone Co., West Virginia." Genealogy Trails. http://genealogytrails.com/wva/boone/vetcensus.html.

Casey, Ada Lynn Hall. "Descendants of William Mullins and Katheryn Smith/Smythe from the Early 1700s." www.rootsweb.ancestry.com/~kyfloyd/familyfiles/mulltree.rtf.

Dilger, Robert J., and Joseph M. White. "Boone County History." West Virginia University Department of Political Science. http://www.polsci.wvu.edu/wv/history.html.

Eastern Digital Resources. "The Civil War in West Virginia." *The War for Southern Independence*. http://www.researchonline.net.

Gross, Larry. "Re: Emmazetta HARLESS-Kanawha or Boone Co/WV." Harless Family Genealogy Forum. http://genforum.genealogy.com/cgi-bin/print.cgi?harless::778.html.

Historical Data Systems. "American Civil War Research Database." http://www.civilwardata.com/.

"Phillip Coon of Coon's Fort, (W)Va and Adam Coon of Boone Co. WV." http://genforum.genealogy.com/coon/messages/3048.html.

Price, O. "Courthouse Burning." Rootsweb. http://archiver.rootsweb.ancestry.com/th/read/WVBOONE/2008-01/1200074883.

"Robert Hager," Biographies of West Virginia Statehood Leaders. Marshall University Humanities Program graduate students, Dr. Billy Joe Peyton's Fall 2010 "Historical Studies" class at Marshall's South Charleston campus, http://www.wvculture.org/history/sesquicentennial/hagerrobert.pdf.

Sahr, Robert. "Inflation Conversion Factors for Years 1774 to Estimated 2013, in Dollars of Recent Years," Oregon State University, http://oregonstate.edu/cla/polisci/sahr/sahr.

Sparks, Martha. "100th Anniversary Celebration." *Logan Banner*. http://loganbanner.com/bookmark/1550415-100th-anniversary-celebration.

West Virginia: The Other History. "Camp Chase Civil Prisoners, 1861–1862." https://sites.google.com/site/wvotherhistory/home.

White, Dustin. "Hallowed Ground: From Cook Mountain to Blair Mountain and Beyond." *Appalachian Voices*. http://appvoices.org/2011/05/25/hallowed-ground-from-cook-mountain-to-blair-mountain-and-beyond.

———. "The History of Cook Mountain." http://www.youtube.com/watch?v=y6JJ3JGjgbU.

Index

About the Author

M ichael B. Graham, PhD, is adjunct professor of history, security and global studies at American Military University, Charles Town, West Virginia. He is senior vice-president for management and chief financial officer at the United States Institute of Peace in Washington, D.C. He graduated from the Air War College and attended the Naval War College and Marine Corps Command and General Staff College, the Foreign Service Institute, Management Concepts Institute, USDA Graduate School and the Academy for Conflict Management and Peacebuilding. He has written or contributed to many books, including *Liberating a Continent: The European Theater* (Vol. 1), *Fall of the Rising Sun: The Pacific Theater* (Vol. 2) and *The Faces of Victory: The United States in World War II* (Addax Publishing, 1995). He authored *Mantle of Heroism: Tarawa and the Struggle for the Gilberts, November 1943* (Presidio Press, 1993), the October 1993 Main Selection/Book of the Month of the Military Book Club.